BREEDING IN CAPTIVITY

BREEDING IN CAPTIVITY

One Woman's Unusual Path to Motherhood

STACY BOLT

Guilford, Connecticut
An imprint of Globe Pequot Press

skirt!® is an attitude . . . spirited, independent, outspoken, serious, playful and irreverent, sometimes controversial, always passionate.

To buy books in quantity for corporate use
or incentives, call **(800) 962-0973**
or e-mail **premiums@GlobePequot.com**.

Project editor: Ellen Urban
Layout: Maggie Peterson

Library of Congress Cataloging-in-Publication Data

Bolt, Stacy.
 Breeding in captivity : one woman's unusual path to motherhood / Stacy Bolt.

  pages cm
  Summary: "More and more women today are waiting to have children—whether intentionally or due to circumstances beyond their control. But when they do, the desire to have a child at an "advanced maternal age" can be both overwhelming and intimidating. Breeding in Captivity illuminates the experience of infertility and adoption, offering readers an inside look at the process while simultaneously captivating them with an extraordinary—often hilarious—story of what it means to become a mother"— Provided by publisher.
 ISBN 978-0-7627-8798-2 (hardback)
 1. Bolt, Stacy. 2. Middle-aged mothers. 3. Infertility—Treatment.
 4. Adoptive parents. 5. Motherhood. I. Title.
 HQ759.43.B65 2013
 306.874'3—dc23

                                                              2013017647

Printed in the United States of America

10 9 8 7 6 5 4 3 2 1

Note to Reader: The names and descriptions of some characters have been changed to protect their privacy.

For Xander

CONTENTS

Part One: Pregnancy 1
Chapter One: Advanced Maternal Age 3
Chapter Two: Her Womb Was a Rocky Place Where His
                    Seed Could Find No Purchase 16
Chapter Three: Bataan Death March Sex 22
Chapter Four: The Spanketeria. 28
Chapter Five: Just Relax .38
Chapter Six: Passport to Certainistan 51
Chapter Seven: FML 60
Chapter Eight: Hearing Voices 62
Chapter Nine: Happy Birthday 68

Intermission 77

Part Two: Adoption 81
Chapter Ten: Keep an Open Mind. 83
Chapter Eleven: Let's Play 120 Questions. 92
Chapter Twelve: Home Sweet Homestudy 97
Chapter Thirteen: The Chosen Ones. 112
Chapter Fourteen: Alarms, False and Otherwise. 118
Chapter Fifteen: Sharp Corners 123
Chapter Sixteen: Meet the Birthparents 130
Chapter Seventeen: Mandatory Waiting Period 136
Chapter Eighteen: Merry Christmas. 148
Chapter Nineteen: Happy New Year. 152
Chapter Twenty: Back in the Saddle Again 159

Chapter Twenty-One: Humoring Crazy People 166
Chapter Twenty-Two: Love Poems and Chili 171
Chapter Twenty-Three: April Fools 177

Acknowledgments 181
About the Author 183

PART ONE: PREGNANCY

CHAPTER ONE

Advanced Maternal Age

It started at the rehearsal dinner. The freaking rehearsal dinner. We weren't even married yet and Dave's Uncle Larry was shouting from one end of the long banquet table to the other, "When're ya gonna pop out some babies?" I was always a big fan of Uncle Larry. He was equally adept at drinking and dancing and, as a result, I always had a great time with him at other people's weddings. But at that moment, I wanted to punch him in the throat.

Turns out Uncle Larry was just the nosy canary in the rude-question coal mine. Over the next forty-eight hours, Dave and I would be asked some version of that same question a dozen times. And why not? People had finally gotten an answer to their previous punch-worthy question: "When are you getting married?" Now it was time for the sequel. Dave and Stacy, Part 2: The Breeding.

The answer to the first question hadn't come quickly. By the time we walked down the aisle, Dave Helfrey and I had been together for seven years. We'd met while working together at an advertising agency. He was a thundering nerd and proud of it. He read comic books, clung to his beloved '80s music, and sported a healthy thicket of dark, Irish curls. He was a cross between Lloyd Dobler from *Say Anything* and Duckie from *Pretty in Pink*. Perfectly imperfect. The only hitch was that he wanted kids someday. And I didn't. Or at least, I thought I didn't.

I was the last of five, born seven years after my closest brother. So my mom had seven long, luxurious years to settle into the idea of never having to be pregnant, give birth, or change a diaper ever again.

And then I came along.

I was the surprise child whose nickname was Whoopsie, and whose existence caused my parents to sever all ties with the Catholic Church and their old-fangled rules about birth control.

So I grew up knowing I wasn't planned, which is different from being unwanted, but only a little. My parents made no attempt to shield me from the knowledge that they'd rather be doing just about anything other than raising yet another child. My father joked about it, because that's what he did. "Well, that's the last time I'll ever have to do that!" he'd laugh when he successfully taught me how to tie my shoes, or ride a bike, or drive a car. My mom just chain-smoked and sighed a lot. That was what parenting looked like to me: exhaustion, exasperation, and benign neglect. Call me crazy, but it didn't sound like much fun.

Years went by—three, four, five of them—and Dave and I were still together. I had all but given him permission to go. But he stayed.

"I'm not in a hurry," he'd tell me when I openly wondered why, if he wanted to be a father so badly, he was still hanging around.

This was, of course, a relief to me. When I tried to picture my life without Dave in it, I couldn't. There was just no other reason to end our relationship. I loved him. He loved me. And the thought of walking away made my insides turn hard.

So I changed my mind. Not immediately, but very, very slowly. Like a bad haircut finally growing out.

I assumed that he would propose immediately. But Dave is a man who needs to come around to an idea. He doesn't jump on bandwagons for the sake of progress. He has to think about it. A lot.

So I began the first in what would turn out to be a very long line of waiting periods. It's worth noting at this point in the story that I am very bad at waiting. When I want something, I want it now. I have no patience for delay. And even after all that's happened, I'm no better at it now than I was then.

In the end, it took him about a year to propose. He promised it would never happen on an obvious day. "You'll never see it coming," he told me, making me wonder if he'd bought a ring or hired a hit man. So when I looked down at my dessert menu on Valentine's Day—the most obvious day imaginable—and saw the words "Queenie, I love you. Will you marry me?" I was indeed surprised. But more than that, I was relieved.

It was finally time to get on with my life.

When I visited my ob-gyn a few months after the wedding and told her I wanted to get pregnant, she delivered one of the least-effective pep talks ever.

"How old are you?" she asked, as I lay splayed out in the cruelly lit exam room, shivering under a thin paper sheet.

"Thirty-five," I said.

"You know that's advanced maternal age, right?" she asked as she warmed a speculum under the tap.

"I'm sorry? Is that, like, an official thing?"

"Yes. It's a thing. After thirty-five, your fertility starts to decline. You don't have as many eggs, and the ones you do have are less viable," she explained, as if to a third grader. "Try to relax. This might be a little cold."

I have to question the humanity of a doctor who delivers this speech while simultaneously giving you a pap smear.

"And if you do get pregnant, you have a higher risk of miscarriage. Down syndrome, too," she continued, peeling off her latex gloves and casually tossing them in the garbage.

"But I just decided to have a baby," I said. "My therapist cleared me and everything. Now you're telling me I can't?"

"Of course not. I'm just telling you that it might take a while. And that it would have been better if you'd decided when you were twenty-five."

"Okay. So. Do you have any advice?" I asked, wrapping the paper sheet around me as far as it would go. It didn't go far enough. "Is there anything we should be doing to help our odds?"

"Have lots of sex?"

"Seriously?"

"Well, yeah. Kind of. My advice is to try on your own for six months. If you haven't gotten pregnant by then, call me and we'll take it from there, okay? Go ahead and get dressed."

Thank you, Dr. Buzzkill.

Advanced maternal age. It sounded like a soap-opera disease. "I'm sorry Jessica, but you have Advanced Maternal Age. You only have six months left to breed." Whatever. I wasn't old. My face was wrinkle-free and I had yet to sprout a single gray hair. "Thirty-five is the new twenty-five," I told my mirror image as I searched for gray hairs.

I went off the pill six months after the wedding. I wanted to start trying right away, especially after being diagnosed as Old. But Dave wanted to wait a year, for a handful of silly reasons that included "We'll be more ready in a year." Six months was our compromise.

I'd been taking the pill and other forms of birth control for nearly twenty years. My fear of motherhood had turned me into the Michigan Militia of contraception. Dr. Buzzkill thought it might take a few months for my body to get used to ovulating again. But it didn't take any time at all for me to return to the violently painful periods that had begun when I was thirteen. Every single month of my adolescence, I'd spent at least two days curled up in a ball, feverish and vomiting. I sat in our family doctor's office and listened to him and my mother talk about what might be wrong with me and what to do about it. He suggested birth control pills as a way to ease the pain and help regulate my runaway periods. Initially, my mom balked. Once a Catholic, always a Catholic. But she finally relented when I was sixteen, worn down by all my whining and wailing. A few weeks after I started taking them, I was thrilled to discover that birth control pills did, indeed, take away the pain. Completely. I clung to that plastic disc of candy-colored pills like a child with a pacifier. And now I was throwing them in the trash because I wanted to get pregnant.

When three months went by without success, I decided to get some backup.

The infertility section at Powell's Books is located between Pregnancy and Parenting. I'm sure someone thought that was a logical placement. It's all about babies, right? But really, it's kind of like putting the books about alcoholism next to the books about cocktail recipes. To make matters worse, the infertility section didn't even take up an entire shelf. There were half a dozen *Oh You Poor, Poor Barren Woman* titles butting right up next to *1001 Awesome Baby Names!*

The book I ended up buying was called *Taking Charge of Your Fertility*. Because taking charge is better than just lying back and waiting for nature to take its course, which, so far, was not working at all.

This book shocked me. Because, get this: *There's a specific way to get pregnant.* And it doesn't involve having sex all the time. It involves having sex at exactly the *right* time. I didn't know this. I really didn't. My knowledge of my own reproductive system was laughable. This is how I remember having The Sex Talk with my mother:

Me: We did Sex Ed in health class today.

Mom: (uncomfortable silence)

Me: They gave me a pamphlet.

Mom: Oh good. Do you, umm, have any questions?

Me: No, I guess not.

The pamphlet appeared to have been printed in 1956. It didn't say anything about getting pregnant. It just told me not to go swimming when I had my period. Plus, I'd been on the pill since I was sixteen, so I never really had to worry about the mechanics of getting pregnant. Not that anyone was trying to get in there. I was a classic vision of awkward adolescence: tall, skinny, glasses, braces, acne. But the fact remains that until I was thirty-five years old, I had no idea that you needed to have sex at the time of ovulation in order to get pregnant.

Taking Charge of Your Fertility completely changed my approach to pregnancy. I was done screwing around, so to speak. Where scented candles and massage oil had once graced my bedside table, now sat ovulation charts, a basal body thermometer, and an increasingly dog-eared copy of the book that had become my personal version of *The Art of War*. Every morning I took my temperature and noted it on the chart. When it started to go up, I knew my body was getting ready to ovulate. When it dropped down, the big event had already happened. And in between those two points, I earned a junior gynecologist's badge for my ability to find and identify the harbinger of impending ovulation: egg-white cervical mucus.

There is no dignity in infertility, a fact I had only just begun to understand.

———

Six months after the Advanced Maternal Age speech, I was back in Dr. Buzzkill's office.

"I think you should see an RE. I can give you a list, but I really recommend Dr. H. He's good," she told me, shoving an oft-copied list in front of me with the doctor's name and number highlighted in acid green.

"RE" stands for Reproductive Endocrinologist. It also stands for Really Expensive. I was hoping to avoid seeing one.

"Why do I need a specialist?" I asked. "Can't you just give me some Clomid?" Clomid is a fertility drug. I'd been doing my research. On the Internet. Doctors love that.

"Sure. In fact, I'm going to write you a prescription for it today. You should take it while you're waiting to see Dr. H. Maybe you'll get lucky and not have to see him at all," she said.

I left her office with a prescription, a phone number for an expensive specialist, and a sinking feeling that my life was about to get a lot more complicated.

Getting an audience with Dr. H was, as Dr. Buzzkill had predicted, difficult. And my impassioned plea to the scheduling nurse ("Don't you understand? My. Eggs. Are. Dying.") was completely unsuccessful. Two months is the standard waiting period for all new patients. During that time, they wanted me to schedule something called an HSG test, which would show whether or not my fallopian tubes were blocked. Then I needed to take the Clomid and chill the hell out for a couple of months.

The HSG test wasn't nearly as "simple" as the doctor's office made it sound. *Simple* is drawing blood and sending it to a lab. Simple does not involve the words "This might pinch a little" while someone inserts a catheter into my uterus. For the record, it pinched a lot. The catheter was used to inject me with a radiographic dye. If my tubes were clear, the dye would flow through them like Porsches on the Autobahn. If they were blocked, the dye would just sit in my uterus—a reproductive traffic jam. The whole thing was broadcast on a flat-screen TV, and as I watched the dye zip through my fallopian tubes, I breathed a sigh of relief and reached for Dave's hand. "Your turn, sport."

I'd spent the last six months toiling in the tedious minutiae of my own fluids and fluctuations. I was the one who did the research, kept the charts, and cracked the completely unsexy whip when it came to having sex. I was the one who got poked, prodded, and catheterized in pursuit of the child Dave and I wanted to have together.

And Dave? He got to jack off with a *Playboy*.

The cruel reality is that male infertility is a lot easier to diagnose. The little soldiers either swim or they don't, essentially. And his did. Swimmingly.

By the time Thanksgiving rolled around, we were almost a year into our attempt to become parents. We spent the holiday with our friends Mark and Rachel, who had eight years of infertility under their belts. Together, they were the Yoda of not getting pregnant. Their home is an elegantly rumpled estate that sits atop Portland's swank West Hills, with a view of the city and, beyond it, Mt. Hood. As friends, they were way out of our league. They drove Lexii and had cocktails with politicians. We took the bus to work and drank during the day. We only knew them because they were friends with my sister Julie. For years we'd all been celebrating Thanksgiving with Mark, Rachel, Julie, and a rotating cast of friends. Dave and I always played the role of interesting outsiders. Over cocktails, we'd regale them with stories of what it's like to wear jeans to work every day. The only thing we really had in common with our hosts was infertility. So on that particular night, I knew I was in safe hands.

In other words, no one was going to ask me if I was pregnant yet.

Most of the people who knew I was trying to get pregnant would look at me expectantly when we got together, raising their eyebrows in some idiotic pantomime of decorum. But others would just come right out and say it.

"So, pregnant yet?"

Why in the name of all that's socially appropriate would anyone ever ask a woman this question? No good can come of it. If I'm pregnant, and I want you to know, I'll tell you when I'm ready. And if I'm not, this question is like getting a drink thrown in my face. It stings. It's embarrassing. And it makes me want to crawl into a corner. Right after I slap you.

That night, I was going to pull Rachel aside and tell her that Dave and I were going to start seeing a specialist. I wanted to get her take on what to expect. But as we sat in their book-lined living room eating fancy things stuffed in endive, they dropped the bomb.

"We're pregnant," Mark blurted out, grinning like a kid in his school picture. "It's twins."

My internal response to the news went something like this:

1. Stabbing pain in my heart and ringing noise in ears. Voice inside my head screaming, "Fuck! Fuck! Fuck!"

2. No, wait. It's Rachel. She's been trying forever. This is good news! Happy! I'm happy!

3. But Rachel was going to be my confidante. She was the only other person I knew who struggled with infertility. Who am I going to talk to now? What about me, me, me?

4. I am a terrible person. I don't deserve to have friends. Or a baby. Where's the booze?

When Rachel left the room to check on the turkey, Mark leaned in conspiratorially.

"IVF with an egg donor," he stage-whispered. "Rachel doesn't like to talk about that part of it."

He was still wearing his school-picture face. The man was giddy.

"Isn't IVF really expensive?" Dave asked. This is not a man who's afraid to ask the rude questions. Had the situation been different, Dave would have been one of the "So, pregnant yet?" people.

"Well, yeah. Of course it is," Mark answered. "But what's another $20,000 when it comes to your kids, right?"

I might have spit out my drink at that point. I'm not sure. Mark was still talking, as oblivious to my shock as only someone who lives on top of a hill could be.

"But the truth is, we owe everything to Dr. H," he continued.

That's where I spit out my drink for sure.

"I'm sorry, who did you say?" I asked.

Mark repeated the name of the doctor we were scheduled to see in just a few weeks, emphasizing each syllable.

"He's amazing," Mark said, leaning back into the soft, over-stuffed couch and rattling the ice cubes in his Manhattan.

I felt Dave's hand grip mine as I told Mark that Dr. H was going to be our doctor, too.

"Well, congratulations," he said, raising his glass to toast us. "Because you're going to get pregnant."

On the drive home, Dave and I were buzzing. We were thrilled that our friends were finally pregnant. And the fact that they'd gotten there with the help of the same RE we were using was just the dark chocolate ganache on the moist, delicious cake of wonderfulness. But the $20,000 comment was sobering. Correction. The *another $20,000* comment.

"Do we want it that bad?" Dave asked as he navigated our banged-up Subaru down the steep curlicue roads out of the West Hills.

"Like, $20,000 bad?" I asked. "I have no idea. How do you put a price on something like that?"

"Easy. You say, we will spend X amount of dollars on this and then we'll quit."

"What do you mean 'quit'? You want to quit? You—"I skidded to a stop just before driving off the "You're the one who wanted a baby in the first place" cliff.

"I don't mean quit trying to be parents," he said, moving quickly to avert my impending freak-out. "I mean quit trying to get pregnant. Maybe we should think about adoption. How important is it for you to carry a baby?"

Beyond the windshield, the night was black and wet. I could see the city lights in the distance. Just beyond them was our home—a small, hundred-year-old Craftsman bungalow. It was a nice place. But it wasn't on a hill.

The wipers swooshed back and forth, clearing and obscuring the view over and over again.

I didn't answer him. I was thinking.

CHAPTER TWO

Her Womb Was a Rocky Place Where His Seed Could Find No Purchase

Sitting in Dr. H's waiting room, it occurred to me that the game had changed. Despite its location in a drab medical building, his office could easily have been featured in *Architectural Digest*. I was used to camping out in Dr. Buzzkill's waiting room, which was littered with old copies of *People*, bright-orange chlamydia pamphlets, and a sad collection of toys that bore the scars of a thousand tiny tyrants. On a battered oak coffee table sat stacks of photo albums with the names of different doctors on the spines. Inside were photos of the babies they'd delivered. Hundreds and hundreds of babies.

But in Dr. H's office, I was offered mineral water with lemon slices while I flipped through the latest copy of *Food & Wine*. There was a fully stocked saltwater reef tank to soothe my jitters and original oil paintings of Tuscany to help transport my bruised psyche to a better, less-failure-tinged place. But best of all: no pregnant women.

They were really starting to piss me off, these women. They were everywhere. And not just strangers, either. Friends, coworkers—even my niece Nicole was pregnant. I would be a great-aunt before I would ever be a mother.

"I'm going to be a great-aunt," I told Dr. H as Dave and I sat across from him in his less-fabulous-than-the-waiting-room-but-still-pretty-nice office.

"And that makes you feel terrible, doesn't it?" he asked, his tone gentle and understanding. This unexpected gesture of empathy was just the thing to let loose the tears that had been building in me for months. I thought of the scene in the movie *Raising Arizona* where Holly Hunter and Nicolas Cage are told they can't conceive. As the doctor tries to explain the situation with a plastic 3-D model of a uterus, a sobbing Holly Hunter barks out, "I'm barren!" Dave and I sometimes acted out this scene during our months of trying on our own. It made us laugh. Now I was afraid I was about to live it.

"Everything about this process is hard. And I'm so sorry that you're going through it," said Dr. H. He handed me a box of tissues, the fancy kind with the lotion infused into the tissues so your nose wouldn't get all red and chapped. This was clearly a man who had sat with his fair share of sobbing women.

Despite the fact that his job was to invade his patients' bodies with all manner of high-tech drugs and tools, there was nothing about Dr. H that was threatening. He was tall and thin, with tousled salt-and-pepper hair and cheekbones that must have been devastating in his younger years. But now, in his fifties, those sharp bones gave him a gauntness that made me want to feed him sandwiches. His voice, like his hands, was soft and feminine. If eye contact were a sport, he would hold the highest title, as well as a lucrative soft drink contract.

As I sat in his office and laid waste to his supply of tissues, any and all reservations I might have had about seeing a Really Expensive specialist dissolved.

"Your HSG test was clear, so that's good," he said as he flipped through my file. "And from the looks of your charts, you're still ovulating regularly, which is great news."

"So why can't I get pregnant?" I asked, eager as always to get to the damn point.

"You probably can," he said. "You just need a little help. Right now I don't see any major barriers. But we're going to do some tests to see what's going on, and then we'll go from there, okay?"

For a former Daddy's Girl, this was exactly what I needed to hear at exactly the moment I needed to hear it. Being the youngest of five children had its advantages. I was "The Baby" and was often treated accordingly, especially by my father. Whether he was conscious of it or not, I think my dad tried to balance my mother's indifference with indulgence. When my car was broken, my dad fixed it for me. When I was having trouble finishing (okay, starting) my topographical map of Oregon for my geography class, he took over the project and got me a solid B. And when my credit rating was in the tank after several terms of wanton collegiate irresponsibility, my dad loaned me the money to set it straight. I was still paying back that loan when he died. But now that The Baby couldn't have a baby, there was no one who could fix it for me. Even if he were still alive, my dad couldn't have done anything in this situation beyond turning beet red and changing the subject.

But Dr. H could. Dr. H was going to fix it.

After our initial chat in his office, he sent me down the hall to change. It was time to take a look at my recalcitrant lady parts. When he said he wanted to do an ultrasound, I imagined every movie / sitcom / soap-opera scene of a pregnant woman getting cold jelly squeezed onto her abdomen and then looking at the monitor to see a fuzzy blob swimming around in her warm, nurturing mommy fluids. But that's what they do with pregnant women. For women like me, who have no blob taking up residence in the uterus, they use a tool that Dave and I immediately christened the DildoCam™.

I liked Dr. H. I really did. But this was, in essence, our first date. And I'm just not the kind of girl who lets a first date violate her with twelve inches of hard plastic. And when he approached me with this high-tech sex toy, which would most likely not be covered by my insurance plan, my knees clamped shut on reflex.

"Don't worry," he said with a gentle smile. "It's not as bad as it looks."

There's an old David Cronenberg movie called *Dead Ringers*, where Jeremy Irons plays psychopathic twin gynecologists. This movie is the reason I insist on having a female ob-gyn. When Dr. H said those words to me he became a psychopathic twin gynecologist. I looked over at Dave and mouthed the words *Dead Ringers*. He doubled over in laughter while Dr. H gently pried my knees apart and sent in the DildoCam™.

Once again, my insides were displayed on a giant TV screen. Dave stopped laughing and stared at it, as he is genetically programmed to do. TV screens are soothing to men, especially when relative strangers are violating their wives with big phallic cameras.

"Okay, everything looks fine," said Dr. H as he slid the Dildo-Cam™ out. "I didn't see any masses, tumors, or cysts."

I didn't know we were looking for masses, tumors, or cysts. I had to process that information before I could feel relieved.

"You go ahead and get dressed and we'll meet back in my office to get a game plan started," said Dr. H, placing a reassuring hand on mine, all traces of Jeremy Irons now gone.

The plan, as it turned out, was for Dave and me to stop having sex. Because clearly, that wasn't working. Instead, we were going to move up to a world of ever-confusing acronyms, beginning with ART—Assisted Reproductive Technology. This is an umbrella term that encompasses everything from Clomid to IVF with an egg donor. My first stop would be a procedure called IUI, or intrauterine insemination. Dave would provide a "sample," a technician would analyze it for sperm count and wash it—whatever that meant—and then Dr. H would inject it directly into my uterus through yet another catheter.

This was supposed to be better than having sex (in a technical sense) because there were more sperm available for fertilization. When it was just the two of us, only the best and the strongest were getting past the gates. Which is to say, not very many. So our chances of succeeding were much higher with an IUI. And really, it didn't seem that complicated. The whole thing would only take a couple of hours and cost a few hundred dollars, which, if it resulted in a baby, was completely worth it. So I left with a new, higher-dose prescription for Clomid and instructions to keep doing my ovulation charts and call when it looked like I was within a day of the Big Event.

I was one step closer to being fixed.

CHAPTER THREE

Bataan Death March Sex

When Dr. H explained the mechanics of an IUI, I was relieved. Not just because someone was finally doing something to help me get pregnant, but because it meant I wouldn't have to have as much sex. The truth is, it was demoralizing. There, I said it. Sex with my husband, who I love more than anyone or anything, had become demoralizing. There was no longer anything spontaneous or light about it. Instead, sex had become fraught with pressure: to get the timing right, to get the position right, to succeed. People who get pregnant easily or accidentally don't understand this. "Well at least you're having fun trying, right?" they'd say to me. And in the beginning, yes, it was fun. "Honey, we 'have to' have sex! Isn't that great?" But as the months wore on, we *had to* have sex. It wasn't fun anymore. And it certainly wasn't romantic.

I once had to borrow a ten-year-old bottle of lube from my mother-in-law. On Christmas Eve. Because I was ovulating.

I never told Dave how much fun I wasn't having while we were trying to conceive. How do you tell your husband that? I didn't have the heart or the nerve to say it. And there was no reason both of us should be miserable. For me, being miserable was starting to become a full-time job. As soon as we started trying, I saw pregnant women everywhere. And at first, it made me happy because I thought I'd be one of them very soon. I smiled at them knowingly, as if we were both members of the same club. I was just waiting for my admissions paperwork to clear. But as my cycles marched on without success, seeing pregnant women stirred up a cocktail of emotions inside me—anger, jealousy, self-pity, sadness, and not a small amount of old-fashioned juvenile petulance. *It wasn't fair!* I wanted to shout, while pounding my fists against the ground. Month after month I was faced with evidence of my failure to fulfill the most simple and natural of biological functions—a function every other woman around me was seemingly able to fulfill without incident. That's when something inside me started to turn.

My friends and family were supportive, always. But I didn't know anyone who had ever gone through the same thing. I needed advice. I needed perspective. I needed a tribe. To find one, I turned to the most logical place I could think of. Because if the Internet can help me find gossip, shoes, and celebrity death hoaxes, why shouldn't it also help me find a few like-minded friends?

There are hundreds of Internet message boards geared toward women who are trying to get pregnant. And while I'm sure they were all established with the intention of giving women support and friendship during what is an undeniably difficult time, I'm equally sure that many of the women who frequent these boards are insane. Interacting with them reminded me of a sorority rush party I went to in college. I'd heard there were free drinks, and I had no money, so I went. Dressed in black and high as a kite, I was set upon by a perky army of Megans and Mollys, all wearing pastel sundresses and coordinating grosgrain hair bows. When they stood together they created a cumulus perfume cloud of Clinique Happy. These were not my people. And no amount of free booze was going to change that.

So it went with the first few message boards I joined.

One of the first signals that I might have accidentally joined Kappa Alpha Fruitcake was the fact that the women who populated these boards referred to sex as "babydancing." Not "doin' it." Not "gettin' busy." Not even good old-fashioned fucking. Nope. They called it babydancing. And when one woman on the board announced that she would be doing the baby dance with her husband that night, everyone jumped in and sprinkled virtual "baby dust" on her.

MAMA2B: YOU HAVE TO STAY POSITIVE!!! ALWAYS!!!

SASSYGURL: NOOOOOO! I will be blessed when it's time! So will yooouuu!!!

MRSH: KEEP THE FAITH GIRL!!!!!!!!!

MAYBEBABY: I am sprinkling tons of baby dust on you RIGHT NOW!!!

Again, I'm sure these were all perfectly nice people who lead productive, happy lives. But, as a general rule, I try not to associate with people who abuse exclamation points and the caps-lock key. There are a handful of people in my life who are exempt. All of them are over seventy and use their computer primarily as a venue for forwarding hyperbolic e-mails about the Democrats' war on religion. These women didn't fall into that category, so I left. But not before announcing that I was divorcing my husband, abandoning my quest for a child, and moving to Bangkok to be a pole dancer. They're probably still talking about me.

My search for a baby-dust-free connection finally ended when I joined the Table Talk message boards at Salon.com. I poked around the Trying To Conceive (TTC) thread and was pleased to find not a single reference to babydancing. Instead, they referred to sex while trying to get pregnant as "Bataan Death March Sex."

Lo, I had found my people.

Joining the TTC board introduced me to a refreshingly bitchy group of women who were going through the same bullshit I was and weren't afraid to talk about it. No one chastised me for not being 100 percent optimistic. No one screamed at me in all caps. It was fantastic. In addition to the usual message-board acronyms, this group had given names to most of the issues and feelings that had plagued me since I started TTC-ing. My favorite was CO/DP, which stands for Cautious Optimism / Defensive Pessimism. This term perfectly described the near-constant tug-of-war that was going on inside my brain as I made my way through each month. It goes a little something like this: You want to be positive. You really do. You want to believe that this cycle, this drug, this procedure will be the one that works. Because if you don't have any hope, then why do it? So you have to be optimistic. But not too optimistic. Because getting your hopes up only to have them smashed back down again? Well, you have to protect yourself. You have to grow armor. So you tell yourself that even though you hope that this cycle, this drug, this procedure is the one that works, you know deep down inside that it probably won't. So you don't get your hopes up. Not too much. Maybe just a little.

Finding a balancing point between Cautious Optimism and Defensive Pessimism is not unlike trying to walk a straight line after drinking an entire bottle of champagne on an empty stomach. You might be able to pull it off once or twice, but eventually you're going to fall on your ass. Dave, bless his heart, did his level best to catch me every time I fell. But he just wasn't as invested in it as I was. How could he be? It wasn't his body that was failing to do what it was supposed to do. He wasn't entertaining the thought that he was less of a man because he couldn't get me pregnant. But I couldn't say the same for myself. I grew up watching shows like *Maude* and *The Mary Tyler Moore Show*. I stole my sister's copies of *Ms.* magazine. I knew, intellectually, that I needed neither a man nor a baby to be a successful woman. And yet, after months of failing to conceive a child, I was seriously starting to question my worth as a woman.

"Are you high?" Dave asked one night after I'd voiced those same questions out loud. I'd just taken and failed a pregnancy test and was spinning the used test stick on our dining room table. "You don't honestly think that, do you?"

"Maybe?" I said. I knew how stupid it sounded. But it felt true.

"This is messing with your head. You're turning into one of those crazy baby ladies," he said. "And please throw that thing away. It has pee on it."

I tossed the test stick into the wastebasket and Dave pulled me onto his lap.

"I'm not a crazy baby lady," I mumbled as I rested my head in the warm crook where his shoulder met his neck. He smelled good, like soap and lasagna. I thought about initiating unscheduled sex. But it seemed like a waste. I wasn't ovulating, so what was the point?

Oh shit. I was a crazy baby lady.

CHAPTER FOUR

The Spanketeria

I've never been a fan of morning sex. Not unless all interested parties agree to brush their teeth first. (I wanted to have that put in our wedding vows, but the priest said no.) So it was with a certain amount of relief that I sent Dave off to submit a sample all by himself on the day of our first IUI.

Sperm are delicate little things. They don't survive in the wild for long, so Dave had to go to Dr. H's office first thing in the morning and use their specially appointed "collection room" in order to give the technicians the freshest possible material to work with. We called this room the Spanketeria. Outfitted with everything a gentleman needs to produce a few teaspoons of life-creating goodness, the Spanketeria was like a miniature version of the Playboy Mansion. Or so I imagined as I was lying warm in our bed and Dave was driving across town on a wet Saturday morning to do the deed. There would be a giant flat-screen TV loaded with the finest porn money could buy. Perhaps there would also be a round bed with satin sheets. And a sexy nurse in a sexy nurse costume would bring in the latest in raunchy periodicals before bidding my husband good luck and leaving to tend to the next brave soldier.

"That sucked," Dave said as he yanked his rain-soaked clothes off and crawled back into bed. His hands were cold.

"No sexy nurse?" I asked.

"I'm sure there's someone in this world who finds that woman sexy. But I'm going to go with mean. And a little scary."

"You sound traumatized," I said, snuggling up to him. His breath was minty fresh.

"She kept knocking on the door and asking if I was done yet."

"Just like me!"

"And the room wasn't nice at all," he whined.

"No round bed?"

"Just a scratchy old couch and some sticky magazines. Clearly, they spent all their money on the lady stuff."

"As it should be," I mumbled, already drifting away. The alarm was set to go off in an hour, when it would be my turn at bat.

Driving to Dr. H's office later that morning, I was a wreck. It was just how I imagined it must feel to drive to the hospital to give birth. Except we were driving to the hospital to get pregnant. I had no idea what to expect. Was it going to hurt? Would I be able to tell right away if it worked? It was so strange, thinking that I could enter a doctor's office childless, and leave it knocked up.

Dr. H himself greeted us in the exam room. It was nine a.m. on a Saturday. Not exactly normal doctor's hours. But, as he explained,

Saturdays were big insemination days. He really said that: "big insemination days." I don't know why Saturday would be any different from other days, ovulation-wise. But it felt nice to be part of something exciting. I pictured him running from exam room to exam room, pushing the plunger to infuse his grateful patients with freshly washed sperm and giving each of them a jubilant high five before moving on to the next anxious mother-to-be-to-be.

But first, I had another date with the DildoCam™. Dr. H wanted to see how many follicles I had and to make sure that I hadn't yet ovulated. He pointed out eight ripe follicles (the structures within the ovaries that produce eggs) and seemed pretty excited about it. Later, when I did some research, I found out that a normally fertile woman has as many as thirty follicles before ovulation. But that would be a much younger woman than me.

Back in the cushy exam room, I felt only the slightest of twinges when Dr. H threaded the thin catheter through my cervix and into my uterus. He was a pro. Dave held my hand as the doctor prepared to inject the sperm my husband had dutifully supplied earlier that morning. We felt like there should be some kind of physical contact between us while a third party attempted to impregnate me, even if it was just some chaste hand-holding. And even though it's standard operating procedure for the two of us to be witty and sarcastic whenever possible, this moment was as serious as it got.

As Dr. H pushed in the plunger, Dave and I held each other's gaze, knowing that this was the moment that could change everything. Forever. He squeezed my hand tightly and kissed my forehead. I pictured the same scene happening nine months later as we waited for our baby to be born.

When it was over, Dr. H told me to stay horizontal for twenty minutes. He dimmed the harsh fluorescent lights as he left and told me to take deep breaths and relax. It reminded me of the old days, when I would stay in bed with a pillow under my hips and my legs hoisted in the air after another round of Bataan Death March Sex. Sometimes Dave would bring me ice cream. Today, we made plans to go out for breakfast.

"I want chocolate-chip pancakes. With whipped cream. And bacon."

"Eating for two already, are we?" Dave asked, still holding my hand.

"And a mimosa. A big one," I continued.

"Shouldn't you be abstaining?" he asked.

"One mimosa can't hurt the little zygote," I said. "Besides, this might be the last drink I get to have for a while."

I stayed on my back for half an hour, just to be safe. Then I got dressed and headed out to the first meal of the rest of my life.

The next two weeks took approximately 125 years to pass. I channeled my nervous energy into a little bit of cooking, some halfhearted housecleaning, and a whole lot of shopping. Normally, I would have been shopping for clothes, but I thought I might be pregnant, so I didn't want to spend money on things I wasn't going to be able to wear in a few months. So instead of stalking the racks at Anthropologie for $80 T-shirts, I went to my Tier 2 Happy Place: Target.

I'm one of those people who can go into Target with three things on my list and leave with a couple hundred bucks' worth of stuff I didn't know I needed, but clearly could not live without. About a week before I was due to take my first official pregnancy test, I found myself in the "Feminine" aisle at my favorite Target, pondering the narrative beauty of the layout. At one end, you have the lubricants and condoms. *Hey beautiful, let's go someplace where we can get to know each other better.* Then you have the pregnancy tests, the STD tests, and the yeast-infection treatments. *Oh shit. Why did I have all those Long Island Iced Teas? And why am I so itchy?* Finally, at the very end are the tampons and maxi pads. *Thank you, God! Thank you! I will never have sex again.* It's an ill-fated hookup played out in the theater of retail. And it was miles away from my own reality. At that point, I would have given anything to get knocked up accidentally. Instead, I was standing there trying to decide between buying a pregnancy test (Cautious Optimism) or tampons (Defensive Pessimism).

I split the difference and bought both.

When I got home and sorted through the mail, I saw that the first bill from Dr. H's office had arrived, and my insurance company wasn't playing ball. The financial counselor had warned me about this. The fact that Dr. H's office had a full-time financial counselor on staff hadn't really registered with me before now. I'd been lulled into ambivalence by the reef tank and the oil paintings. Looking over the bill, I understood how they were able to afford the reef tank and the oil paintings. And the fancy tissues with the lotion.

Every single point of contact between myself and Dr. H's office was itemized on the bill:

- Initial consultation with Dr. H
- Two sessions with the DildoCam™
- Analysis of said DildoCam™ sessions
- Sperm analysis
- Sperm washing
- Phlebotomist for my blood work
- Lab fees for analyzing my blood work
- Intrauterine insemination

I was surprised they didn't include a rental fee for the Spanketeria. The entire bill was a little over $1,000, all out-of-pocket.

Dave and I had been self-employed for a few years at this point. Or, as our parents liked to call it, unemployed. The year we got engaged, the ad agency where Dave and I worked went out of business when the so-called Dotcom Bubble burst. Dave was one of the founding partners and the failure of the company hit him hard. Being a partner in a successful agency was a point of pride for him. Partly, I think, because it was something his father could understand. Dave's dad was a chemical engineer with little patience or understanding for his artistically inclined only son. But owning a business was something he could point to and say, "My son does that."

After the agency closed, Dave took a long time to figure out what he wanted to do next. He and I both knew that whatever it was, it wasn't going to be a traditional advertising gig. He was thirty-eight years old and a certifiable creative genius (if such things could actually be certified). Advertising is no place for creative geniuses. Mildly creative people like myself can do very well in advertising, but creative geniuses always end up getting their spirits killed and their souls sucked out, hyperbolically speaking. Advertising had broken Dave. He needed to find a brand-new path in life. I only needed to find a slightly different one.

For me, the transition from employed copywriter to freelance copywriter was pretty seamless. Not being part of a day-to-day office job was a welcome change. I was sick to death of office drama and ladder climbing. And the love affair I'd had with advertising had long since died. I studied it in college at my dad's urging. I'd wanted to be a writer. As in, a Real Writer who wrote Important Things. He wanted me to stop borrowing his money. So I got a BA in advertising, thinking I would get a job at an agency and then work on my so-called "real writing" at night. Instead I got sucked into the ultracompetitive, hyper-creative Portland ad scene of the '90s.

I wouldn't write a word that wasn't used to sell a product or service until I was almost forty.

By mid-2001, I'd lost my office job and most of my professional ambition. I just wanted to make the largest amount of money for the smallest amount of effort. Working as a freelancer, it turned out, was the perfect solution. Ad agencies were willing to pay me $600 a day to do work that was ridiculously easy. Freelance copywriting paid for our wedding and our honeymoon. It paid the mortgage and the utilities every month. And it paid for the tens of thousands of dollars' worth of medical bills we were about to rack up.

Getting an official pregnancy test from a doctor does not involve peeing on anything. That's the good news. Instead, blood is drawn and quickly processed. Definitive answers are given in a matter of hours. One does not have to stand under a fluorescent bathroom light trying to figure out if there are two lines or just one while simultaneously trying to avoid getting pee on one's hands. In this new world of Assisted Reproductive Technology, there are no lines. Just needles.

"You should just go on about your day like you usually do. We'll call you in a few hours with the results," the nurse said.

Her name tag said Joyce and had little smiley-face stickers all over it. Joyce had just filled a vial with my blood and was now taping a cotton ball onto the inside of my elbow.

"I've already taken seven tests," I told her. "They were all negative." Joyce made a snorting noise that seemed to indicate that I'd flushed $42 worth of pregnancy tests down the toilet.

"Those things are notoriously inaccurate," Joyce said, prying the little squeezy ball out of my hand and putting it back in the drawer. "This is the best way to know for sure."

Behind her was a bulletin board covered with snapshots of babies. Dozens of babies. Not hundreds like in Dr. Buzzkill's office. We were no longer concerned with quantity. Although there were several sets of twins and triplets. SUCCESS STORIES! the board proclaimed. I smiled at the pictures and felt a fluttering in my stomach.

Even with the seven minus signs decorating the bottom of my bathroom wastebasket, I knew I was pregnant. I was having crazy mood swings. My boobs were swollen and sore. I'd had some low-grade nausea for the last week or so. Those were all symptoms of early pregnancy. I knew that because I'd spent many otherwise billable hours researching the signs of early pregnancy on the Internet. I had even managed to get three people on the TTC board to agree that I might be experiencing some symptoms of early pregnancy and therefore I might be pregnant. But that's all they would agree to. They're bitchy like that.

"So when you say 'a few hours,' do you mean three hours exactly? Or maybe sooner?" I asked, gathering my purse and coat.

"Hard to say," Joyce said with a smile. "We'll get to it as fast as we can."

This poor woman dealt with Crazy Baby Ladies all day, every day. I was just one of dozens she'd see that week. And to each of us she probably said the exact same thing: Just go on about your day. We'll let you know.

Words like these do nothing to help the crazy. In fact, they only make us crazier. Go about my day? Was she fucking kidding me? I wasn't waiting to hear if I had strep throat; I was waiting to hear if I was pregnant.

At home, I pretended to work on an ad for a teeth whitener. The client wanted to know if there was a "more interesting" way to say "whiter teeth." Clients were always asking stupid questions like that. "Is there a better way of saying 'good'?" "Is there a newer way of saying 'new'?" I pulled up the thesaurus widget on my computer and typed in the word *white*. It came back with *chalky, milky,* and *snowy.* Nope. There was not a more interesting way to say "whiter teeth." I noted on my timesheet that I had spent two hours searching for an alternate way to say "whiter teeth." Suck it, hand that feeds me.

I looked at the clock on my computer. Then at my watch. Then at the clock on the wall. *This is torture,* I thought. Cruel and unusual punishment. I even picked up the phone to make sure it was working. I thought people only did that on TV. But here I was, picking up the—JESUS CHRIST ON A CRACKER!

The phone rang. It scared the shit out of me.

"Hello?" I said, mopping up the growing pool of Diet Coke I'd spilled on my desk.

"Hi, this is Joyce from Dr. H's office. Is this Stacy?"

"Yes, it is," I said. *Ka-thump. Ka-thump.*

"Well, your blood test indicates that you are not pregnant this time," she said, her voice rising in pitch ever so slightly. She must hate this part of her job.

"Oh. Are you sure?"

"Dr. H wants you to do another IUI cycle with Clomid. We called the prescription in to your pharmacy. Call us when you're about to ovulate, hon."

After I hung up the phone I sat at my desk for a while, watching the dark brown soda seep into the creative brief for the teeth whitener. Diet Coke stains your teeth. Did you know that?

I went upstairs to pee. I sat there looking at our black clawfoot tub and imagined myself bathing a giggling child in it. I looked down and saw a dark red bloodstain in my underwear.

Period. End of sentence.

CHAPTER FIVE

Just Relax

Four IUIs later, I still wasn't pregnant. After Joyce called with the last negative pregnancy test, she told me Dr. H wanted us to make an appointment to "come in and chat."

Oh goody.

I was pretty sure this was going to be the IVF talk. And I wasn't ready to have the IVF talk. I wasn't ready to be the woman who needed IVF. Because that woman has problems. Big ones. I was just having a teensy little problem getting pregnant. And why not? It took me forever to decide to have a baby, so why wouldn't it take forever to get pregnant?

I have a thing for symmetry. And rationalization.

I called and made the appointment for the end of the week. As I listened to the hold music ("Spring," by Vivaldi? Please!), I stared at the crystal ice bucket on my kitchen counter. It was full of tiny bottles of liquor. It was a "sorry you're not pregnant but at least you can still drink" gift from my three best girlfriends, Pat, Courtenay, and Marie. Dave referred to us as the Coven. They'd presented me with the bucket of booze after my third IUI had failed. It was easily the best, most thoughtful acknowledgment of what I was going through to date.

Infertility is kind of like having a death in the family: Everyone feels bad for you but no one knows what to say. Especially if they've never experienced it themselves. In all the years Rachel was trying to get pregnant, I don't think I ever said a word to her about it. That's one of my family's signature traits: It's better to say nothing than to say the wrong thing. In terms of fucked-up Bolt Wisdom, it's second only to "If there's a chance you might fail, why try?"

Then again, maybe the Bolts have a point. Because, to be perfectly truthful, the people who said nothing were far preferable to the people who said stupid things.

And there were a lot of those people.

"You know what you need to do, honey? Relax. Just relax."

I was at a cousin's wedding and I'd been cornered by a family member who shall not be named.

"Really," I said, with a complete lack of inflection. This was not the first time I'd been offered this particular nugget of wisdom. It wasn't even the fifth time. I'd actually lost track.

As a server walked by with a tray of champagne, I grabbed a glass and took a long swallow.

"Absolutely," she continued. "I was having the hardest time getting pregnant. And then I just stopped thinking about it. I said to myself, just let go. Stop worrying. And bam! I was pregnant with this one."

She was holding her four-month-old son in her arms. It was her third child. He looked like Mr. Magoo.

"How long were you trying?" I asked.

Wait for it.

"Four. Months."

Here we go.

"Wow. That long."

"Mmm-hmm. It was brutal. I know exactly how you feel," she said.

Rise above it. Rise above it. Rise above it.

"Okay. Well. I'm going to go find Dave. You take care," I told her as I started to back away, scanning the room for another tray of champagne. I wanted to drink the goddamned stars.

"You too," she called after me. "And remember: Relax!"

Shut up, you fucking cow. You have no idea how I feel. Why? Because you have a baby, you idiot. If you've been pregnant three times, you have no idea what it feels like to not be able to get pregnant. If it took you four months to conceive, you have no concept of what it feels like to watch fifteen months go by without success. And if five IUIs, eight rounds of Clomid, a Really Expensive doctor, and a fifth of gin can't get me pregnant, I don't think "just relaxing" is going to do it either. But thanks for your utterly baseless, medically retarded, and deeply insulting advice nonetheless.

Of course, I didn't say that. Not out loud, anyway. The people who said this to me (and there were many) didn't mean to be idiots. They meant well. They were trying to help. And in every single case, they were friends or family, so I didn't really have the heart or the guts to unload on them.

But sometimes, I really, really wanted to.

The idea that a woman's ability to conceive is somehow related to her level of anxiety isn't new. But it is stupid. Infertility is a complex medical condition that could be caused by a vast number of factors. Telling an infertile woman that she just needs to relax is, in essence, telling her that it's her own damn fault she's not getting pregnant. That the solution to her problem is somehow in her control. That she's just not trying hard enough. Or maybe, just maybe, that it's all in her head.

I have no doubt that there are women who have succeeded in getting pregnant after deciding to "just relax." But I don't believe for one minute that that's the reason they were successful. They got pregnant because they were able to. Because there were no underlying medical conditions getting in the way. Because they weren't infertile.

Just like the people who tell the bereaved that their loved one is "in a better place," or that "God had a plan" for them, the people who tell infertile women that they just need to relax aren't helping anything. A simple "I'm sorry" works wonders. So do tiny bottles of liquor. Or maybe they could take a page from my family and keep their fool mouths shut.

Portland's Pearl District is home to trendy boutiques, of-the-moment restaurants, ridiculously overpriced condos, and Dr. H's office. On the day that Dave and I arrived for our "chat," there were no parking spots. And too many pedestrians. And several of the smug, overconfident bicyclists that rule Portland's streets.

I wanted to kill each and every one of them.

"Relax, sweetie. Just relax," said Dave, patting my knee.

I wanted to kill him, too.

Dr. H was running late, so we took our seats in the waiting room. It no longer had the calming effect it once did. (Fuck you, fish tank.) I scanned the room and immediately picked out the new kids. They held hands and looked hopeful. There was still money in their bank accounts. They were probably still having sex.

Just wait.

When it was finally our turn, we were ushered into the doctor's office and he shook our hands. (Really? A handshake? This is a man who has tried to impregnate me five times. Shouldn't we at least be on fist-bump terms by now?)

"So," he said, looking me straight in the eye.

"So," I said, ready for battle.

The night before, Dave and I had had a long talk about IVF. Neither of us was crazy about the idea. Dave called it the "Frankenbaby" option. I thought that was a little harsh. My concern was more about the cost of the procedure. And the invasiveness. And the risk of multiples. I wanted one child. I did not want a litter. IVF felt, to me, like a natural stopping point. But I wasn't ready to give up, either. We hadn't even gotten into the serious fertility drugs, for instance. What about using those with IUI? What about alternative therapies? I wasn't about to get railroaded into an expensive procedure just so Dr. H could buy more fish.

I could almost hear my father whispering that idea in my ear: "Don't let him try to sell you something you don't need!" He was wary of the world, and of salesmen in particular. Maybe because he'd been one for so long. He taught all of us not to trust anyone who's trying to sell you something, which is rich considering he was the person who steered me into advertising. Even after he was dead, when my brothers and my sister and I went to the funeral home to make the arrangements, we were prepared for battle, because that's what he'd taught us. Dad wanted to be cremated, and we assumed, based on years of training, that the funeral director would try to sell us on an expensive coffin and burial plot. But he didn't. He just did what we asked and offered lots of tissues. We didn't know what to make of it. Years after my father's death, I'm still surprised when people don't try to take advantage of me.

"This isn't working out very well, is it?" Dr. H asked, smiling his smile.

"Not yet," I said.

"I've been reviewing your charts from your ob-gyn. How long have your periods been painful?" he asked.

"From the beginning, pretty much. Why?"

"I think you might have something called endometriosis."

He explained what it was, but later I had to look it up on the Internet. I don't speak doctor. Basically, endometriosis is when the tissue that normally lines the uterus—the endometrium—starts growing outside the uterus. It still acts like it normally would: It thickens, breaks down, and bleeds with each period. But because the tissue has no way to exit the body, it gets trapped and starts irritating the surrounding tissue, causing scars and adhesions to develop, which, in turn, can cause infertility. Some women never have any symptoms from endometriosis, but some have insanely painful periods. Like me.

This conversation answered a question I'd been asking since I was thirteen years old.

"So, how do you know for sure if I have it?" I asked.

"We'll have to take a look inside," Dr. H said, folding his hands in front of him like a politician at a podium.

"Oh. Okay. Can we go look right now?" I asked, thinking he'd just whip out the DildoCam™.

"When I say 'take a look,' I mean surgically," he said. "That's the only way I can know for sure."

"Surgically? Like, with surgery?"

"That's generally how we do it, yes."

Despite the sincere and applied efforts of my three barbaric older brothers, I'd never been in the hospital. Never broken a bone or had stitches. And I'd certainly never had surgery. The idea terrified me.

"Can't you just give me a prescription to clear it up?" I asked.

"No," he said, the hint of a smile breaking across his face. "Surgery is the only way to confirm it and the only way to remove it. If it makes you feel better, this would just be laparoscopic. No big incisions. You'd go home the same day," he said, continuing to court my vote.

"Will you put me under?" I asked.

"Yes," he said.

"Will you cut me open?"

"In a manner of speaking, yes."

"Will you sew me back up?"

"Of course."

"Then I don't feel better."

The car was silent on the drive home, but it was noisy in my head. I was turtling. This is Dave's term for how I deal with stress. I disappear into my own brain and conduct emotional, illogical, and generally psychotic conversations with my various head voices. There's no point in talking to me until I decide to come out. So he just drove.

The introduction of surgery into the equation had thrown me for a loop. Back when it first became obvious that I was going to need some help getting pregnant, I pictured pretty much the exact same scenario I had already experienced. Just a lot shorter in duration. I expected to be rounding the corner of my first trimester by now. Back in July when I'd bought tickets to see U2 in December, I had smiled at the thought of my child attending that concert in utero. Now, not only was I not going to be smuggling another person into the show, but I didn't even have a reasonable expectation of success. According to Dr. H, if I decided to go ahead with the surgery, it would be scheduled for January. I'd need to take a week off from work to recuperate, and then a couple of months off fertility drugs before we were cleared to try again.

That meant another Christmas would go by without a baby.

The holidays suck for the infertile. Wherever there are large gatherings of family, there are people who want to know if you're pregnant yet. And if you're not, they want to give you stupid advice. Holidays also carry the curse of sentimentality. If you're one of us, you fantasize about announcing your pregnancy at the crowded Thanksgiving table, or at your family's big drunken Christmas party. Cheers will erupt and champagne will be opened and passed to all but you, the blessed mother-to-be. And everyone will be so happy for you.

But while you're waiting for your chance, you have to watch others do it instead. Cousins and sisters and, yes, even nieces all make their big announcements at family gatherings. And you put on your I'm-so-happy-for-you face and try not to make eye contact with your husband, because if you do, you might just start crying, and that would make you infertile *and* pathetic. So you take consolation in being able to drink that glass of champagne that the mommy-to-be can't have. In fact, you have two. Maybe three.

Oh hell, give me the damn bottle.

It's hard to close the door on the idea of never making that announcement. But that's just what I was trying to do on the drive home from Dr. H's office that day. I was trying to close the door. Because the moment the word *surgery* came out of the good doctor's mouth, this process officially became Too Fucking Hard.

The sick truth is, even after months of fertility treatments, I was still afraid of pregnancy. I was afraid of it in the same way I was afraid of broken bones and stitches and surgery. It was a fear of the unknown and the unpleasant. I'd always thought that it was tied to my fear of motherhood. But not long after I started seeing Dr. H, I was revisited by a recurring dream that I used to have back before I wanted a child, when I used enough birth control to stop twenty women from getting knocked up. In the dream, I'd be rubbing my big, round belly with maternal pride. But then I'd feel something touching my hands from the other side and when I looked down I could see two little talons reaching out and stretching my skin like a cheap piece of spandex. Not sweet little baby hands, but claws, tearing me apart from the inside.

Back then, when I'd wake up from this dream, I'd just roll over and say a quiet "thank you" to the good people at Ortho-Novum for sparing me the horror of pregnancy. But now, months into my fertility treatments, I had to ask myself: Do I really want this? And the answer was always the same: Yes, I do. I want a child. More than anything.

The question I should have been asking was: Do I really want to get pregnant?

"I want to quit," I told Dave that evening as we were sitting on the couch watching *Lost*.

"Me too," he said. "This sucks. Too much talking, not enough Smoke Monster." He pointed the remote at the TV and fired it like a gun.

"Not the show. The treatments," I said. "I want to quit the treatments."

"Quit?"

"Yes."

"You want to quit?"

"Yes."

"Okay," he said, picking up the remote and turning the TV back on.

"Hey!" I grabbed it out of his hand. "What the hell?"

He was silent for a second. Gathering his thoughts.

"Well, it would appear that you've made the single biggest decision of our lives without bothering to talk to me about it first. So as long as I'm completely irrelevant, I might as well see how this ends," he said, gesturing toward the screen.

Dave is calm and logical. He is pragmatic. It makes me insane.

"I don't want to have surgery," I said, tears pooling in the corners of my eyes. I hate crying.

"I know you don't," he said, turning to me and taking my hands in his. "But that's a different issue. Not wanting surgery and not wanting to keep doing fertility treatments are two different things."

"This is so hard," I said.

"Of course it is," he said. "It's the biggest thing we'll ever do. What makes you think it should be easy?"

"It's easy for everyone else! It's easy for Nicole. It's easy for my friends. It's easy for the crack ho down the street. Why can't it be easy for me?"

"There are no crack hos on our street."

"You know what I mean."

"Yes, I do. But so what? So what if it's easy for other people?"

"It's not fair."

"No. But it's not high school either, sweetie. Fair doesn't matter. It is what it is."

"I don't want to have surgery," I said, again.

"I don't blame you. But laparoscopy doesn't actually sound all that bad. It's not like they're going to open you up. They're basically just poking a couple holes in you and looking around," he said, petting my hair. I'm such a sucker for hair petting.

"What if it works?" I said, almost under my breath.

"You lost me," he said.

"What if the surgery works and I get pregnant?"

"Then . . . yay? Isn't that what we want?" He was speaking slowly, as if to a crazy person. Which is exactly what I was.

Before this talk with Dr. H, my problem had been vague and undefined. We weren't sure why I wasn't getting pregnant. Let's try this. Let's try that. But once he brought up the endometriosis and the surgery, I had a diagnosis. And a potential cure. This might really happen. I might really become a mother. Someone should put a stop to this.

Dave looked me in the eye.

"We need to get you off these drugs, sweetie. They are messing with your head. We already covered this. Remember? You will be a good mother. People do this all the time. And you can, too. And besides," he continued, "even if the surgery doesn't help you get pregnant, wouldn't it be worth it to never have to be doubled over with cramps again?"

Goddamn pragmatic asshole.

The pre-op waiting room was ice-cold. They made me wear a plastic hair bonnet. And it was 6:30 in the morning. We were not off to a good start. But when the IV nurse finally showed up, she came bearing Valium.

"I heard you might be a little nervous," she said, handing me a tiny paper cup containing two peach-colored pills. "These should help."

And they did. Fantastically. I didn't even notice when she started the IV. I was in Happy Town. At one point, I declared to Dave that if the procedure worked, I wanted to name our child Valium. Valium Helfrey.

Later, as they wheeled my gurney down the hall toward the OR, Dr. H walked by and waved at me like he was on a parade float.

"See you in there, kiddo," he said.

Kiddo?

Inside the bright, cold operating room a scrub nurse covered me with a warming blanket which, combined with my double dose of Vitamin V, made everything okay. Sure, I was splayed out on the operating table like Christ on the cross. And yes, I was about to have my reproductive organs examined and possibly scraped out in order to make room for a baby, which may or may not want to tear me apart from the inside. But none of that mattered because I was toasty warm and flying high.

When the anesthesiologist came in, I thought he had a Dean Martin quality to him: tan and carefree and maybe just the tiniest bit drunk. Not necessarily what you want in an anesthesiologist. But I was past the point of no return. He lowered the clear plastic mask over my nose and I breathed the medicated air deep into my lungs like a bong hit.

"Relax, Stacy," he said from far, far away. "Just relax."

CHAPTER SIX

Passport to Certainistan

My first clear postsurgical memory is of sitting on a toilet in a relentlessly bright hospital bathroom while a nurse was trying to attach a maxi pad to my underwear. For a minute or two, I thought I was back in college. The pad, she told me, was to catch the "debris" that would be coming out of me for the next week or so. I was still suspended in the fog of Dr. Dean Martin's expert anesthesia, so I was unable to register the two reactions that should have come immediately: 1) Why is a total stranger putting a maxi pad in my underwear? and 2) Debris?

Back in my bed on the recovery ward, Dave was reading a comic book and I was slowly coming out of it when Dr. H popped his head in.

"How are we feeling?" he asked, perching on the edge of my bed.

"We're feeling funky," I replied. "How did it go?"

"Outstanding," he said.

What was originally scheduled to be a "quick peek" into my reproductive system to look for endometriosis had turned into a four-hour surgery in which years and years of scar tissue and adhesions were lasered out of me. The official medical description was "excision of extensive and severe endometriomas." Dr. H referred to it as "striking gold."

"We found the problem and we took care of it," he told me. "Now we can get serious."

I hadn't realized we'd been pretending.

Back at home, I took to my bed like a tubercular eighteenth-century heroine. I had stacks of books and magazines to leaf through, courtesy of the Coven. I had an iPod loaded with every cheesy feel-good song I could download. And I had Percocet. God, I loved Percocet. I called them my "perks" because that's what my dad had called them when he took them. He'd look at his watch and say, "Time for my perks!" After a certain point (post-chemo, pre-morphine), his perks became the highlights of his day. They were staving off the pain that was radiating from inside his bones, where cancer was eating away at them like termites, slowly but surely bringing down a proud old house.

My pain, of course, was different. And nowhere near as bad. But taking the pills made me feel a posthumous allegiance to him. They also made me feel like singing "Shipoopi" from *The Music Man* every hour, on the hour. So maybe I shouldn't attach too much meaning to any of it.

On day three, Dave left for the grocery store. I needed a change of scenery. Lying in my bedroom only made me want to rearrange the furniture, which is something my husband would say I do compulsively. I can't really argue. When I had mono in the eighth grade, I missed a month of school and had to lie in bed much of the time. One afternoon my mom came into my room to find my white-and-gold Montgomery Ward bedroom furniture completely rearranged and me passed out on the floor. In my defense, it really opened up the room. But a four-hour abdominal laparoscopy does not lend itself to furniture moving, so I opted for some TV instead.

I shuffled into the TV room and gingerly parked myself in a straight-backed chair. Even with the Percocet, getting up from any position was an expletive-laden exercise in pain, so it was best to take the path of least resistance. The couch, while luxuriously comfortable, was out of the question, as it was at least a decade old and had the structural integrity of a beanbag chair. Even if I managed to get in, I'd have to call 911 in order to get out.

Flipping around, I stopped on a rerun of *The Daily Show*. Big mistake. Laughter? Not the best medicine in this case. So I switched to *Matlock*, which, for some reason, immediately made me feel the need to pee. Twenty minutes later, as I was sitting on the toilet, I looked down and screamed. My once-white winged maxi pad was now black. *What the fuck?* And then I remembered: This was the debris I'd been warned about by the nurse. And she was not kidding. It looked like the stuff that bubbles up from the drain after you plunge it out. It was pitch-black and evil—the remains of whatever didn't get suctioned out of me during my surgery. And while it was completely disgusting, I was also thrilled to see it. Because it was evidence of success. It was the black sludge of hope.

Throughout the week, friends and family came to visit, all of them telling me what I already knew: The wait was over. I was going to get pregnant. I knew this like I knew my own name. This knowledge was like being in a strange, exotic country whose language I didn't speak, but whose culture was intoxicating. Certainty is not my thing. I doubt the weather report, the numbers on the scale, and my husband's love for me in equal measures. My entire life, I have never been sure of anything. Except this. And now that I'd experienced it, I wanted to apply for citizenship in the land of Certainistan.

Three months later, after enduring the mandatory postsurgical waiting period, I arrived at Dr. H's office for my sixth IUI. I sailed through the door and into the waiting room with smiles of beatitude for all the waiting couples. "Don't worry," my eyes told them, "your time will come, too." As Dave and I waited to be called back, I gazed at the fish tank.

"We should get one of these," I told Dave.

"That's a $15,000 saltwater reef tank," he said. The words *you moron* were not spoken, but they were implied.

"Well, it doesn't have to be this fancy," I said, undeterred. "But don't you think it would be great for the baby?"

The baby. It had always been "a" baby. Now it was "the" baby. What a difference an article can make.

The next day, after dutifully resting post-IUI, I was standing in the middle of our small sunroom, planning. The crib, I thought, would go against the far wall, the only one without windows. It gets cold in there in the winter, and I didn't want the baby to get a chill. The changing table would go against the window that looked out onto the garden. I thought it would be nice to look at something scenic while cleaning up baby poop. I imagined the walls painted daffodil yellow, with bright white trim to match the furniture I'd picked out online the day before. The crib and changing table were in the Jenny Lind style, with turned posts that gave them an old-fashioned look without any of that old-fashioned lead paint. I added them to a gift registry I'd just started, but hadn't yet published. There's a fine line between confidence and hubris, and I was determined not to cross it. (I'll admit to being just superstitious enough to believe in a link between hubris and bad luck.) I hadn't given myself permission to buy anything baby-related because that seemed like hubris. But now, at least, I felt like I could start looking at things. That seemed okay.

I also decided it would be okay to start excavating the sunroom. For five years it had been our Dump Room—the place where we put everything we didn't know what to do with. Dave and I are both very acquisitive people. We buy things and collect things and gather things for God knows what future scenario. We once joked that if we ever formed a band we'd call ourselves "The Borderline Hoarders." Going through this room was like an archaeological dig of our recent past.

I squatted down and grabbed a wrinkled brown shopping bag. Inside were four pairs of my skinny jeans. Size six. I put them in a pile of things to get rid of. If I wasn't a size six before pregnancy, I wasn't going to be one after. Underneath the bag was a stack of white boxes. I opened them and found the inhabitants of the Island of Misfit Wedding Gifts. I hadn't had the heart to throw them out. You never know when you might need a porcelain music box with a picture of the Pope on it, right? But now it was time to get serious. We were going to need this room. As if on cue, I heard a rustling sound behind me. I turned and looked into the crooked, slimy eyes of Elvis.

When we first moved into the house, Dave had a small, weird menagerie comprised of a black king snake named Snowball, three geckos, and Elvis the iguana. Elvis was the only one left. I consider myself an animal lover, and I love having pets. But I draw the line at pets that require other pets for food. The day I discovered a Tupperware container full of baby mice in our freezer was the day Snowball was introduced to the good people of Craigslist. And the geckos, cute as they were, ate live crickets. Which are gross. So Elvis the herbivore was the last of the exotic pets. He lived in a cage that had been constructed before he'd reached his full size. Now, at more than five feet long, including his tail, the poor thing was cramped and grumpy. Elvis needed a new home. And I needed a nursery that didn't have a reptile in it.

I summoned Dave to the Dump Room.

"New project!" I said, sounding like a cross between a cheerleader and a preschool teacher.

"Oh yeah?" Dave asked, skeptical.

"We need to clean this room out. Now."

"Why?"

"Elvis needs to go someplace else," I said.

"Why?"

"Are you kidding me?" I asked. The preschool teacher had left for the day. And the cheerleader, as we all know, was really a bitch.

"I don't—"

"You don't really think it's okay to have an iguana in a baby's room do you?" My voice was rising in pitch with every syllable.

"Wait. What?"

"Dave. This is not acceptable. You have to do something about this."

"Eventually, yes, we do need to do something about Elvis," he said, very slowly. "But we don't even know if you're pregnant."

"Yes, we do," I said.

"Honey."

"Yes. We. Do," I said, handing him a bag of old comic books.

Dave doesn't believe something until he sees it. And he had not seen an official confirmation of my pregnancy; therefore, it didn't exist. Therefore, the sense of urgency I was feeling was not his problem. Besides, he was otherwise occupied with his new business venture. He'd finally discovered his new path in life: Halloween.

For as long as he could remember, Dave had been obsessed with Halloween. He loves it like I love Christmas. At the agency, we hadn't held an annual Christmas party; we'd had an annual Halloween party instead. Dave would spend months constructing the props and decorations, oblivious to the fact that most of the people attending the parties were far more concerned with whether or not it would be open bar. The fact that the vampire skeleton thingy had an animatronic armature (or something) was lost on them.

One evening while we were talking about what he should do next, I casually threw out the idea of turning his obsession with Halloween into a career. Within a few weeks, he'd struck up a friendship with the owner of a haunted house that was put on every year at the Jantzen Beach SuperCenter shopping mall in Portland. He'd offered Dave a small corner of his real estate to create his own "haunt" in October. That was six months away, and Dave had thrown himself into the task with the kind of enthusiasm I hadn't seen from him in years. In many ways, I was thrilled for him. Sure, this was a risky venture that might not pan out, and it wasn't exactly the direction I'd imagined our lives taking when we got married. But he was happy, so I was happy. Except for the part where he refused to do anything to help me get the nursery ready.

Dave had not followed me on my journey to Certainistan, so he was not motivated to drop everything else on his plate in order to do what I wanted him to do. This bugged the living shit out of me, because I knew that even when we got our pregnancy confirmation (which would be any day now), he would take most (if not all) of the ensuing nine months to get off his ass and clean out his stuff, living and otherwise.

I could picture myself in the beginning stages of labor, bag packed and standing by the door, while Dave carefully sifted through every comic book and placed each one in a protective plastic sleeve.

"Do we have to go right now?" he'd ask. "I'd really like some more time to go through these."

"You had nine months to go through them," I'd say, through clenched teeth.

"Your water just broke," he'd say, not even bothering to look at me. "We've got, like, *hours* before anything really happens. You worry too much."

And then I would kill him. Not with my bare hands, because I would be too fat to reach down to where he was squatting on the floor amongst his *X-Men*. Instead, I would knock him down with my overnight bag and then I would step on his throat, unleashing the full force of my pregnant fury, not to mention my considerable weight, on his fragile windpipe.

I really hate it when things don't go my way.

CHAPTER SEVEN

FML

BOLT 9:22am: Today's the day, girls. I go in for the preg test at 10. I should get word around 1-ish. If any of you sprinkle baby dust on me I'll hunt you down and hurt you.

JULIA 9:23am: Fine, no baby dust. But how about some genuine good thoughts? All of that and more coming your way today, toots.

MEG-O-MANIAC 9:25am: Same here, Bolt. Happy thoughts. White light. Whatever floats your boat. I just want to hear some good news today.

IZ 9:25am: Go Bolt Go! I really want you to succeed today. Mostly because I want you to move to another board. Bitch.

BOLT 11:07am: What time is it?

IZ 11:12am: Not time yet. Go look at kitten pictures.

MEG-O-MANIAC 11:15am: Did you get the good nurse this time, Bolt?

BOLT 11:17am: Ahhh, yeah. Joyce has the magic touch. Didn't feel a thing. Or maybe I'm just getting used to having my blood sucked out.

JULIA 12:37pm: Hey, Bolt, I have champagne chilling in my fridge. Seriously. And you can't have any. Because you're pregnant.

BOLT 12:40pm: I could have a little sip.

JULIA 12:51pm: See? You're already a bad mom.

BOLT 12:56pm: J What time is it? :-)

MEG-O-MANIAC 1:22pm: Anything? Anything? Bolt? Helllooooo?

JULIA 1:25pm: It's quiet. Too quiet . . .

IZ 1:27pm: She's celebrating. Without us. Get the baby dust.

BOLT 1:32pm: Hi, girls.

MEG-O-MANIAC 1:33pm: And? So? What's the news?

BOLT 1:34pm: Fail.

JULIA 1:35pm: Oh shit, honey.

IZ 1:35pm: Fuck. Really?

MEG-O-MANIAC 1:35pm: (((((Bolt)))))

BOLT 1:37pm: Can I have that champagne now, Jules?

JULIA 1:38pm: You can have anything you want, doll.

BOLT 1:40pm: No, I can't.

CHAPTER EIGHT

Hearing Voices

I closed my laptop and listened.

You can't do this.

Oh, good. I was hearing voices.

You should stop trying.

Not now, please.

This is the Voice that has been whispering to me all my life. It's how I was raised: If there's a chance you might fail at something, don't try. When I was a teenager, I was terrified of public speaking—so much so that I concocted all manner of outlandish excuses to avoid reading out loud in class. But I had an English teacher who saw through my bullshit and made me do it, over and over again. And the more I did it, the better I got. Eventually he convinced me to try out for commencement speaker. My school didn't automatically give the job to the valedictorian; they gave it to the person who wrote and delivered the best speech. When I told my parents, their response was, and I quote: "Why would you do something like that? What if you don't get it?"

For the record, I did get it. And I was great, despite a complete lack of encouragement from my family. But that's how we are. We don't put ourselves out there. We don't do things that are hard, or that might cause us pain or suffering. And, as the Voice had lately been reminding me, my current situation was rife with pain and suffering. It was harder than hard.

The Voice had a point.

— ◦ —

"This is not the time to give up," Dr. H said. He'd asked us to come in after we got the news about the pregnancy test. Now he was trying to talk me off the ledge.

"We did the surgery," I said. "You got the endometriosis. You said we were all clear. Why didn't I get pregnant?"

"All this tells me is that it's time to bring in the big guns," he said.

This comment upset me for two reasons. The first is that I did not appreciate the phallic imagery, thank you very much. Please keep your dick out of my reproductive folly. And second, if we must use phallic imagery to describe these increasingly unnatural methods of conception, wouldn't the guns in question have been the surgery I'd just recovered from?

"For the next IUI, I want you to do a round of injectables," he said. "That should get us the results we're looking for."

So the guns in question were injectable hormones designed to simulate the natural process of ovulation and produce lots of fat, happy follicles. Bang bang bang!

The first set of shots would contain HMG, or human menopausal gonadotropins. (Fun Fact: These drugs are made up of hormones extracted from the urine of postmenopausal women!) After taking the HMG injections for seven to twelve days, I would get a so-called trigger shot of HCG, or human chorionic gonadotropin. This would stimulate the follicle(s) to release the egg(s), which would be met by my husband's sperm via IUI. HCG, you might be interested to know, is derived from the urine of pregnant women. Never underestimate the power of pee.

"What happens if the shots don't work?" Dave asked.

"If this doesn't work, then the next logical step would be IVF," he said.

It was the first time he'd used that term with us.

We told Dr. H we'd call him the next day and let him know whether or not we wanted to do the shots. He looked a bit like a child who's had his toy gun taken away. But this was a turning point, and we needed to figure out where to go next. On the drive home, Dave kept one hand firmly planted on my knee, a gesture that translated roughly as, "I am here for you. Please feel free to turtle as needed."

But I wanted to talk. It was time.

"I'm really sorry," I said.

"For?"

"Being defective. If you'd married Elizabeth, you'd have a kid by now."

Elizabeth was Dave's ex-girlfriend.

"Actually, if I'd married Elizabeth I'd have eight kids by now. I'd also be working as an associate brand manager for Procter and Gamble and playing golf every Saturday," he said, swerving to avoid mowing down a smug bicyclist.

"Your point?"

"Is that I would be miserable in that situation," he said.

"But you'd be a father," I said.

"Not relevant."

"But—"

"For better or worse, baby. In sickness and in health."

"What should we do?" I asked, resting my throbbing head against the cold window of the car. I couldn't remember not having a headache.

"What do you want to do?" he asked.

"I'm tired."

"I'll bet you are," he said. "You've been through a lot for a person who never wanted kids in the first place. And if you wanted to quit right now, I wouldn't blame you. Unless you wanted to quit because you've been listening to the Voice."

Dave knew about the Voice. Dave hated the Voice.

"The Voice is an asshole," he said. "And it's wrong. You *can* do this. It's just a question of whether or not you want to."

"I know," I said, as we sailed over the Fremont Bridge with the dark waters of the Willamette River churning below us. It was early spring in Portland, which meant that the damp, cement-colored gloom was occasionally interrupted by big honks of yellow from the wild daffodils that were popping up everywhere. *Hang in there,* they seemed to be saying. *It's almost over.*

"How do you feel about adoption?" I asked, breaking the silence.

"The same way I always have," Dave said. "I think it's great."

"But do you think it would be great for us?"

"I do."

"Would it bother you that the child wouldn't be . . ."

"Born of my genetic cesspool? No, honey, it wouldn't. Would it bother you?"

"I think the world would probably be fine without another passive-aggressive Bolt."

"Agreed," he laughed. "But do you think you'd be okay with never being pregnant?"

"Have I told you about my recurring dream?"

"Yes, and I'd love to develop a horror-movie script about it someday. But for today, let's figure this out."

We drove and talked. We went to lunch and talked. We went home and talked. For the rest of the afternoon and into the night, Dave and I hashed out our future as parents.

Adoption had come up many times over the course of our journey toward parenthood. I was always surprised that Dave reacted as favorably as he did. I've known a lot of couples who were split down the middle when it came to adoption. And in every single case, the partner who didn't want to adopt was the man. I'm not going to try to attach any kind of larger sociological significance to this, because, clearly, my control group is way too small. But it's interesting nonetheless: The women were willing to forego pregnancy in order to become parents, and the men weren't. I've known women who, like me, wanted to stop at IVF but whose husbands pushed them to do it. If that's not a deal-breaker, what is? But

Dave, my wonderful, amazing, openhearted husband, had always viewed adoption as a healthy, viable alternative to the bullshit we were currently going through. "If there are children in the world who need homes," he'd say, "why not give them one?"

Why not indeed?

As the night wore on, Dave and I were circling in on what, in retrospect, was such an obvious choice. But we weren't quite ready to make it yet. It's hard to close the door on the image of yourself with a big, round belly that total strangers want to touch because it's life itself that you're holding inside you. It's one thing to say you're going to go as far as IVF and then stop. It's quite another to actually do it. Because when you go through month after month after month of trying to get pregnant, how do you just stop? How do you know that the next time wouldn't have been The One?

But it had to stop somewhere. For two years, we'd invested our hearts and our money in hopes of getting pregnant. That might not seem like a long time on paper, but it's an eternity when you measure it in two-week increments.

The next day I called Dr. H's office and told them we wanted to go ahead with the shots. The nurse faxed me an order form and two prescription slips. The form was for a pharmacy in England that sold the HMG and HCG. It was much cheaper that way, she told me. Then she scheduled a training session for Dave and me, so we could learn how to do the injections. I hung up the phone knowing we had a plan.

CHAPTER NINE

Happy Birthday

"This drug is called Pregnyl. Seriously."

The injectable drugs had arrived from the pharmacy in England, and Dave and I were getting ready to do the first shot.

"There's another one called Fertinex!"

In my work, I am occasionally called on to name products. I've come up with names for a line of fancy coffees and some children's games, among other things. The process can be long and arduous, with legal teams and approval committees and the CEO's nephew all weighing in with their opinions. How, I wondered to myself as I leaned over the counter with my pants pulled down, did Pregnyl ever make the cut?

"I would have called it 'KnockUp,'" Dave said, taking out a Sharpie and putting a small black dot on my upper-right butt cheek. "But I'm not a copywriter."

"No, you're not. I think they should call it 'Expensivan,'" I said, as I was looking over the invoice for the drugs. It was a mortgage payment, plus shipping. And this was the cheap option.

On the kitchen counter we had spread out all the paraphernalia we needed to do the injection: alcohol, cotton balls, a syringe, a vial of HMG, and a red medical waste container. Seeing all of this stuff next to our pink stand mixer and the cookbooks I would someday open and use, I was struck by the absurdity of it all. The stand mixer had been a wedding gift from the Coven, something I imagined using to make elaborate birthday cakes for my child. The cookbooks were all about creating healthy meals for kids. Look how far we hadn't come.

"Ready?" Dave asked, hoisting the syringe in the air like Eric Stoltz in *Pulp Fiction*.

"Oh yeah, baby. Give it to me good. Stick me with your big long needle," I said, still looking at the invoice.

During our training session, Dave practiced giving the injections to oranges. He needed to get comfortable with the idea of having a needle in his hands, the nurse told us. I was perfectly comfortable with a syringe, having had a diabetic cat for two years, but I couldn't inject myself without some serious contortions. So it was up to Dave.

I didn't really see a lot of discomfort from him. In fact, he seemed alarmingly comfortable with the idea of stabbing me with a sharp object. Which made a certain amount of sense. He'd put up with his fair share of histrionics from me in the last two years. He'd dutifully attended every ultrasound, every IUI, every chat with Dr. H. He'd given me pep talks when I needed them and he'd patted my sobbing head every time I hit the wall. Infertility isn't just hard on women, and a lot of couples don't survive it. But Dave had been a champ. And now he was about to stab me in the ass with 30ccs of Pregnyl.

For better or for worse, indeed.

There were only a few people who knew we were doing the shots: Dave's parents, my sister Julie, the TTC board, and the Coven. I had long since stopped telling my mom what was happening. She never asked because she didn't like to pry. She was the daughter of a notoriously nosy woman, and it was her life's mission to be the opposite of her mother. But the opposite of nosy is apathetic, which is how my mother often seemed to me. When I offered information about what was going on, my mother didn't give me pep talks or tell me to hang in there. She told me there was no shame in quitting. "Why are you putting yourself through this?" she'd ask. "Maybe it's just not meant to be."

You can't do this. You should stop trying.

What I lacked in maternal support, I more than made up for in drunk girlfriend support. The Coven had followed every twist and turn of the journey so far, and when we started doing the shots, they summoned me for an "emergency shindig." I arrived at Marie's apartment to hear the three of them whispering and giggling in the kitchen.

"Don't come in!" they shrieked when they heard the door close behind me. So I parked on the sofa, put my feet on the surfboard-shaped coffee table, and turned on the TV. A few minutes later, the three of them emerged from the kitchen wearing pink feather boas and bras on their heads. Pat was carrying a silver serving tray containing a plastic turkey baster, a Twinkie, a white candle, some deviled eggs, and another bra. She put it down on the table and the three of them knelt down in front of me, their faces full of mock solemnity. Clearly, they'd gotten a head start on the drinking.

"What the fuck is all this?" I asked.

"Fertility ritual," they said, in unison.

My memories of that night are unreliable, because there were large amounts of champagne dispensed through the turkey baster. Marie has pictures that show me with a bra on my head. I can assume that the eggs and the Twinkies were consumed and the candle was blown out with the requisite wish for a bun in the oven. But I don't remember any of it. Nor do I remember what Court's friend Keith told me that evening. Keith is a psychic and came over to do readings for the four of us. According to Pat, Marie, and Court, he told me that there was a baby in my future, that it was a boy, that he wasn't my biological child, and that he wasn't coming anytime soon.

It's certainly reasonable to assume that I don't remember Keith's reading because I was drunk. Then again, I remember the things Keith told my three friends about their pasts and futures. Court was going to marry the man she'd just broken up with. Pat had been a rat in a previous life. Marie was a prostitute who'd died of an STD. But when I try to remember my own reading, there's nothing there. It's like it never happened.

———

I had ultrasounds and blood tests every few days during that cycle, so Dr. H could monitor the growth of my follicles as well as my hormone levels. When it was time to do the trigger shot, he was optimistic. As luck would have it, my last IUI would take place on May 23—my thirty-eighth birthday.

This would be my seventh IUI. Dave was meeting with his new business partner about the haunted house, so he couldn't be there for the actual insemination, but he'd done the important part, so I didn't mind handling the rest on my own. It had become routine at that point. We were old pros. I didn't even really care that Dr. H couldn't be there. He was speaking at a medical conference, so his partner Dr. X stepped in. As I lay in the stirrups waiting for him to insert the catheter, he looked over my chart, including the blood tests from the day before that charted my hormone levels.

"Huh," he said, frowning.

"Problem?" I asked.

"Yeah. Your levels are bad."

Dr. X did not possess any of Dr. H's kind demeanor. He was terse and impersonal. I couldn't imagine going through this process with him.

"My levels? What levels?"

Dr. X peered over the clipboard and fixed me with a look that said, "Are you a fucking idiot?"

"All of them, sweetheart," he said, in what is possibly the most condescending tone I've ever heard. "The ones that should be high are low and the ones that should be low are sky-high. We can do this if you want, but I'd wait another month and try again if I were you."

He had no idea what those words meant to the person hearing them. Wait another month and try again? Shell out another

$8,000? Get my hopes up just to have them smashed by some asshole who'd rather be golfing? There was no way in hell I was going to do this again.

"Just do it," I said, laying back and closing my eyes.

My uterus had become a Nike commercial.

On my way out, the nurse scheduled an appointment for a pregnancy test in two weeks. Then she asked if I'd like to settle my bill.

"How much?" I asked.

"It's $2,752—not including today's procedure."

I gave her my credit card and paid it off. As I was leaving, she called out to me.

"Hey, happy birthday, sweetie! Have a great day!"

That afternoon, Dave and I got a kitten.

We'd been planning it for a couple of weeks. My beloved Zooey the diabetic cat had died the year before, and I was finally ready to get another one. I still had Nancy, the cat I'd had since college. But she was old and cranky and hated Dave. Even after years of living with him, she'd still hiss every time he walked by. Since Zooey died, she'd gotten worse. Having a kitten in the house, I reasoned, would mellow Nancy out and give me a warm, fuzzy distraction. I'd found the kitten on a pet-adoption website. She was a brown tabby just like Zooey, and she'd been dumped at a local park when she was only a few weeks old. The fine human being who had done this had tied her up inside a pillowcase and thrown her out the window of a moving car. Someone at the park saw it happen, so the kitten was taken to a shelter right away and nursed back to health. When I got home from the IUI there was a voice mail from the shelter. She was finally ready to come home with us.

Having a fluffy kitten to play with salvaged what might have gone down as the worst birthday ever. And it made my final two-week wait go a lot faster. We named her Chopper, for no good reason other than the fact that it amused us. I bought her a soft bed and lots of toys and took pictures of her constantly. She had become my stand-in baby. Sharp syringes in my backside were replaced by fierce little kitten claws issuing adorable puncture wounds all over my body. Crazy pee hormones were supplanted by purr-induced calm. Maybe I don't really need a baby, I thought as Chopper slept on my shoulder. Maybe I could just be a crazy cat lady.

It was pregnancy test day. My very last one. The attendant waved to me as I pulled into the parking lot of Dr. H's office. I was a veteran. I didn't even need to be escorted to the blood-draw room anymore. I knew exactly where it was. Two rights and a left.

Inside, Joyce was waiting for me.

"We've got to stop meeting like this," she said with a wink.

As she filled the vial with my blood, I stared at the wall of success stories behind her. Every time I came in, there were more photos. This time, Michael and Maya were there, Mark and Rachel's twins. I'd first met them when they were about a month old. Rachel and I sat together in the nursery for a long time. She was breastfeeding Maya and I was holding a sleeping Michael. We were both quiet, hypnotized by the tiny miracles in our midst.

When Rachel finally spoke, it startled me.

"This is the most amazing thing I've ever done," she said. "You have to do this, Stacy. You just have to." She never took her eyes off Maya.

"Well, we're working on it," I said absently, as I stroked Michael's impossibly tiny head.

Rachel leaned forward and put her hand on my knee. She looked at me with an intensity that was actually frightening.

"Do whatever you have to do," she said. "Whatever it takes."

"Okay, you know the drill," Joyce was telling me as she taped a cotton ball to the crook of my arm. "Lots of tests today, so I'll probably call you mid-afternoon with the results."

She helped me get my raincoat on and then she gave me a hug. She'd never hugged me before.

"I'm pulling for you, sweetie," she said.

I thanked her and left.

Afterward, I was killing time at Fred Meyer, a local retail chain that sold everything from groceries to sporting goods. I normally hated going to the one by our house because it was so huge. Dave and I called it the Mothership. But it had one of the best wine departments in town, so I went there to stock up every couple of weeks. On this day, I was in the champagne aisle.

A bottle of Argyle sold for $24.99. That was more than I usually paid for champagne, but this was going to be a special occasion, one way or the other. As I reached for the bottle I could feel the cotton ball that was still taped to my arm. There was just the slightest twinge of pain beneath it.

Once home, I put the bottle in the fridge. By the time Joyce called with the results, it would be nice and cold. If the news was good, I would invite my friends over to drink it in my honor. If the news was bad, I would open it and drink it right then and there.

Dave was in an all-day meeting, so I had the house to myself. I stretched out on the couch with Chopper and turned on the TV. I was sound asleep when the phone rang. It took me a second to remember where I was or what was going on. But then I remembered. It was Joyce with my test results.

I answered the phone.

When I hung up, I popped the cork and drank the cold champagne straight from the bottle.

Intermission

Some people say dealing with infertility is like riding a roller coaster. I call those people hacks. Really? A roller coaster? How original. But that's the thing about clichés: Just because they're boring doesn't mean they're not true. When you're infertile, you start every month full of excitement, anticipation, and maybe even a bit of fear as you begin the long climb toward ovulation. And when you finally reach the top you can see everything in front of you: your pregnancy, your baby, your whole life as a mother. Then your period shows up and you plummet straight down at 40 mph, leaving a trail of empty wine bottles and compound expletives in your wake. So yeah, it is a roller coaster. And in many, many ways, I was relieved to finally be off of it. But that doesn't mean I took the decision to stop treatments lightly.

When we went in for a "postmortem" appointment with Dr. H, I was still feeling conflicted about quitting. I'd managed to close the door most of the way, but it was as if the wood had expanded on a hot day, and no matter how hard I shoved, I just couldn't get it to close all the way.

"What about IVF?" I asked him, while Dave patiently held his tongue.

"Honestly? I don't think you'd be a good candidate. Not unless you were willing to consider an egg donor," he said.

After that, there was a whole bunch of medical gobbledygook I wish I could remember, but I can't. It's gone. I think my brain had absorbed all the medical information it was capable of retaining and the rest just dribbled out onto Dr. H's expensive carpet. But really, he'd already told me all I needed to hear: *I don't think you'd be a good candidate.* It silenced the chorus of what-ifs that had been playing in my head ever since I'd sobered up from my champagne bender. It also helped to validate the crassly practical calculation Dave and I had worked out a few weeks before: Stay with infertility treatments and maybe get a child. Switch to adoption and definitely get a child. Both options involved lots and lots of money. But only one had a guaranteed outcome. It wasn't pretty or romantic. But it was our reality.

So we thanked Dr. H for all his help, paid our bill, and shoved the door shut.

After a six-month break from all things baby, in December of 2005, I made another pilgrimage to Powell's Books. Back when I'd started looking for help getting pregnant, I was indignant at how few books there were on such a complex subject. By contrast, the adoption section at Powell's was vast. There were dozens of books about every facet of adoption: international, domestic, infant, older child, special needs, adoption through agencies, adoption through lawyers, open adoption, closed adoption, bonding with your adopted child, not bonding with your adopted child, and on and on and on.

As I stood there cradling a stack of books roughly the size and weight of a healthy baby, I heard a sound behind me. It was far away at first, but it was coming closer and closer. It sounded like a train, but not quite, and it was slowing down right behind me. The brakes squealed, the sounds stopped, and I turned around.

It was a shiny new roller coaster.

I took a deep breath and climbed on.

PART TWO: ADOPTION

CHAPTER TEN

Keep an Open Mind

It had been three months since I'd stood in Powell's with an armload of adoption books.

When we were going through infertility treatments, there were no guarantees that anything we tried was going to work. But with adoption, we knew that when we came to the end of this particular obstacle course, we would have a baby. The sense of freedom in that knowledge was intoxicating. There was, it seemed then, no wrong answer. We chose domestic adoption instead of international because we knew we were only going to do this once. Even before we had started trying to get pregnant, Dave and I knew we only wanted one child. And if we were going to adopt, we wanted to be with our child from the very beginning. International adoption simply did not afford that opportunity. We were told that the youngest baby we could expect to adopt would be about six months old. And even that was rare.

We chose an agency in Portland that specialized in domestic adoptions. My friend LeeAnne had adopted both her children through them and had nothing but praise for the agency. Dave and I liked them because they were the only agency we interviewed that focused solely on domestic. We attended about a half-dozen open houses for different agencies, all of them held in bland hotel conference rooms with stale coffee and fluorescent lighting. After writing our names on stick-on tags and grabbing an information packet, we'd take our seat among the other nervous parents-to-be—mostly straight, white couples, some singles, a few gay or lesbian couples. Then the lights would go down, the tender Sarah McLachlan music would begin, and the heart-tugging video would play.

From one open house to another, the videos were the same: images of children waiting—waiting in cold metal cribs, in derelict yards, in ramshackle huts. "These children are waiting for you," the person in charge of the presentation would say. And the couples would look at each other and hold hands. Then the agency would bring in someone who had successfully adopted an adorable child from China or Russia or Guatemala. "Look," they seemed to be saying as they held up their child for the childless to see. "Look what you can have."

During the Q-and-A period, the agency reps would go around the room and ask which country people were interested in adopting from: China? Russia? Guatemala? When we said we were interested in a domestic adoption, we got variations of the same response: "Oh. We can do that, too. If you want."

By contrast, the agency we chose did nothing but domestic adoptions. And they'd been doing it for over a hundred years, so there was no fly-by-night, take-the-money-and-run kind of vibe like we'd gotten from some of the other places. They were honest, straightforward, and welcoming. Their goal, they told us, was to find families for children, not the other way around. Other agencies treated us like customers in the shoe department at Nordstrom: *What kind of a child are you looking for? Dark? Light? Healthy? Slightly damaged? If I don't have what you're looking for in China, I can always call Guatemala.* For them, it was a business transaction.

So it was refreshing to meet with people who weren't really interested in catering to our needs. They were doing it for the children. And they weren't doing it for a profit. After the financial bruising we took during the infertility treatments, Dave and I were wary of the costs of adoption. We'd heard horror stories about birthmothers demanding tens of thousands of dollars and then changing their minds. Our fears weren't eased by the cagey nature of the other agencies we met with. No one seemed willing to give us even a ballpark figure of how much we were looking at. "It varies," was all they would tell us. Our agency, on the other hand, charged a flat fee of $25,000. Not a small sum by any means, but it was payable over time at different milestones in the process. And it was finite. If, for example, the birthparents changed their minds, we would still pay the fee only once.

"Does that happen often? The birthparents changing their minds?" Dave asked.

"No, not often. But it does happen, and we want our prospective parents to be prepared for that."

We were sitting in the offices of our brand-new adoption agency on a rainy March afternoon. It was a standard-issue drab gray conference room. The overhead fluorescent lights were off, which made one mushroom-colored surface blend into the next. Outside the picture window was a view of the iconic wooden water tower in the John's Landing neighborhood, and, beyond that, the mud-choked Willamette. March has to be the most depressing month of the year to live in Oregon. Winter is mostly over, but warm, dry weather is still so far away. And in between, you're faced with a relentless string of cold, rainy, gray days.

"So, what brings you here today?" asked Meg, the adoption clinician who was doing our initial interview. She was a classic Portland hippie: salt-and-pepper hair wound into a loose bun, baggy purple sweater, floor-length peasant skirt, Birkenstocks with thick socks.

"We'd like a baby, please," Dave answered. "Do you have any we can take home today?"

She gave him a patient smile that said *I'll tolerate your inappropriate humor. For now.*

"Okay, let me rephrase that," she said. "What led you to adoption?"

"The usual," I said. "I couldn't get pregnant. That is the usual, isn't it?"

"It's very common, yes. But it's not the only reason people adopt," Meg said.

"No, of course not. I just meant—"

"Are you still trying to get pregnant?" she asked, with just a hint of accusation in her voice.

"No."

"Because you need to tell us if you are. We need you to be one hundred percent committed to adoption. This can't be your backup plan."

"We are. One hundred percent. Committed, I mean," I said, my cheeks blooming red.

Never piss off a hippie.

"Okay. Well. My notes say that you're interested in an infant adoption. Is that right?"

I nodded. Not speaking seemed like a good idea.

"Have you thought about the degree of openness you'd be comfortable with?" Meg asked. She was talking about open adoption, an arrangement in which the birthparents stay in contact with the adopted child.

"If we said none, would that be a deal-breaker?" Dave said.

"With us? No. But it might be for the birthparents. We strongly advocate for open adoption, and most of the birthparents who come to us want some degree of openness from the adoptive parents. If you choose not to have an open adoption, you might be waiting a long time."

The concept of an open adoption was terrifying to us. It meant that the birthparents would be in our lives, to some degree or another, for the rest of our lives.

But despite our discomfort with the idea of open adoption, it had become the accepted standard for domestic adoptions. And when you compare it to the way adoptions used to be handled in the United States, it's hard to argue with the idea. I have a cousin who got pregnant in the early 1970s. My aunt and uncle, being obedient Catholics, whisked her off to a home for unwed mothers before anyone could notice she was expecting. Everyone in the family was told that Dee was attending boarding school on the East Coast. Instead, she was living out the last months of her pregnancy among a bunch of mean old nuns who took her baby away as soon as he was born and gave him to a childless couple. The adoption was sealed and everyone was told to go on with their lives. That's how adoptions were handled for the better part of the twentieth century. There weren't always mean old nuns, but the records were always sealed, and the adoptive parents were usually instructed to behave as if the child had been born to them.

Adoption was a dirty word.

Open adoption came out of the backlash that happened when the children who had been placed in closed, sealed adoptions began demanding to know where they came from. Proponents of open adoption will tell you that it benefits all the members of what's referred to as the "adoption triad," meaning the birthparents, the adoptive parents, and the child. But most of all, the child.

"Can you tell me why you're resistant to the idea of an open adoption?" Meg asked.

"I worry about boundaries," I said hesitantly. I didn't want to piss her off again.

"How so?" she asked.

"Can the birthmother just come by anytime she wants? What are our rights as the adoptive parents?" I asked.

"As the adoptive parents, you are the sole legal guardians of the child. The birthmother—and the birthfather, if he's in the picture—signs away all parental rights when she signs the adoption agreement. You will be the parents of the child. Period. An open adoption simply means that you agree to share photos and updates with her throughout the year, and that you will have an agreed-upon number of supervised visits per year."

"And who decides that?" I asked.

"You and the birthparents decide together. She can't come over anytime she wants unless you agree to that kind of arrangement," Meg said. "And for the record, we don't recommend it."

"Why not?" I asked.

"It's not healthy for anyone. But I think it's especially confusing for the child. The vast majority of open-adoption agreements we see have no more than two visits a year."

"Huh."

"What else can I tell you?" Meg asked.

"You mentioned the birthparents changing their minds," Dave said. "How much time do they have to do that?"

"Once the papers are signed, there's no going back."

"So the birthmother can't come back in six months and take away the baby?" I asked.

She smiled a humorless smile. "I know there have been a few well-publicized cases where that's happened, but Oregon law doesn't allow it. There is no so-called 'waiting period' here."

"Apparently, everything I know about adoption comes from *Lifetime* movies," I said.

Meg put both hands on the table, lacing her bony fingers together.

"It can be a scary idea at first. I know that," she said. "But I really believe that open adoption is the best thing for an adopted child."

When we got home I called LeeAnne—my friend who had recommended the agency—and grilled her about open adoption. Dave listened in on the other line.

"It definitely took some time for us to get used to the idea," she told me. "But after a while, we realized that the reality was much less scary than what we had imagined."

"So how often do they see their birthparents?" I asked.

"Now? Hardly ever. But when they were little, we'd meet with them a couple of times a year. They'll call the kids on their birthdays and we still send them pictures, but they've really faded into the background as the kids have gotten older," she said.

Talking to LeeAnne made Dave and I feel a little bit better, but we still weren't completely comfortable with the idea of an open adoption. Of course, we had long since passed the point where we could reasonably expect to be comfortable with anything. Nothing about the process so far had been easy. Why should this?

——◦——

We signed with the agency in March 2006. For the next couple of months, we worked on something called the "homestudy," which is really a whole bunch of paperwork, a two-day training seminar, and one actual visit to study your home. The paperwork consisted of a detailed financial statement to prove economic stability, an FBI criminal background check, a series of personal references, and a questionnaire containing a whopping 120 questions about everything from our parents to our relationship to our positions on discipline.

I'm pretty sure that no one who has ever gotten accidentally knocked up while on a three-day meth binge had to answer 120 essay questions about their potential as a parent or submit to an FBI background check.

But maybe they should.

CHAPTER ELEVEN

Let's Play 120 Questions

This questionnaire was designed to help us gather some basic facts about you and to give you an opportunity to share your thoughts and feelings about your life. This information is critical in helping us understand what your strengths are and how you have resolved difficulties in your life. We hope that this questionnaire will also help you think about issues that might arise in your future parenting efforts. All information is confidential and will be used solely for the purpose of completing the adoptive home study.

Q: When and why did you first begin thinking about adoption?

A: Please see chapters 1 through 9.

Q: How did you arrive at the decision to adopt?

A: Please see pages 77 through 79.

Q: How have you resolved the loss (or potential loss) of your biological child?

A: Slowly, and with large amounts of alcohol.

Q: What scares you most about adopting?

A: Answering 120 questions about adopting.

Q: How were affection, anger, and sadness expressed in your family?

A: Affection: Rarely

Anger: Passive-aggressively

Sadness: Keep it to yourself

Q: What would you change about your childhood?

A: I would go back in time to the night my brother Eric and I were watching *Sanford and Son*. I was six and he was thirteen. This time, when he gets up to go to the bathroom I will refrain from changing the channel to *Charlie's Angels* so that when he comes back into the room he will not fly into an adolescent rage and scream, "THERE IS NO SANTA CLAUS!!"

Q: What is your happiest childhood memory?

A: The day Eric moved out and I got his room.

Q: How do you deal with negative feelings or down times in your life?

A: A bottle of wine and Zappos.com.

Q: In what ways have you changed over the years?

A: I've gotten taller. And fatter. I have more wrinkles. My hair is turning gray. My eyesight is worse. My wardrobe is better. I changed my mind about wanting a child. I discovered that I couldn't have a child. So now I'm adopting a child. Also, with time and reflection, I've come to understand that George Harrison was the best Beatle.

Q: What type of discipline system will you implement as an adoptive parent?

A: Guilt.

Q: How do you emotionally support your partner?

A: I compliment him on the size of his penis. I also pretend to agree with him when he claims that graphic novels are a legitimate form of literature.

Q: What characteristics of your partner do you believe need improvement?

A: I believe his iguana-removal technique could use a great deal of improvement. He disagrees.

Q: What was the most stressful period of your relationship, and how did you handle it?

A: I'll let you know when it's over.

Q: Under what circumstances would you seek counseling for your child/family?

A: Setting fires. Having violent outbursts. Liking reggae.

Q: How could a child most easily upset you, and how will you handle it?

A: There is nothing my child could ever do to upset me, because I plan to be on Valium for the duration of his or her childhood. Hey, if it's good enough for my mom, it's good enough for me, right?

Q: What kinds of activities do you enjoy as a family?

A: Paying fertility bills. Talking about infertility ad nauseam. Talking about adoption ad nauseam. Harping about the state of the "nursery." Ignoring the harping about the state of the "nursery."

Q: What kinds of activities do you enjoy separately from your partner?

A: Getting drunk with my girlfriends and complaining about my partner.

Q: What is your relationship with religion?

A: We're no longer on speaking terms.

Q: With whom have you discussed your adoption plans?

A: Family and close friends. And, of course, you.

Q: What responses have you received regarding these plans?

A: Here are the current Top 3 Hall of Fame Responses:

1. The real mom will just take it back. I saw a movie where that happened.
2. You won't be able to love it as much as you would your own child.
3. You know what's going to happen now? You're going to get pregnant! And then you'll have a real baby!

Q: How will you discuss adoption with your child?

A: We will tell our child that she was purchased from the police, and if she misbehaves we can return her for a better child.

Q: What do you think makes adopted children want to find their birthparents?

A: Having adoptive parents like us.

CHAPTER TWELVE

Home Sweet Homestudy

It took Dave and me about two months to finish our respective questionnaires. Despite my initial desire to respond to each question in the snarkiest way possible, I took the job as seriously as I could and answered as honestly as I felt comfortable. But it was hard, because I knew that someone was going to take that information and use it to evaluate my fitness as a parent. You want to make yourself look good. But not too good. For example, I told them that I shoplifted a watermelon Lip Smacker in the eighth grade because, in the grand scheme of things, it's not that bad, and it makes me look human. But I didn't tell them I flunked out of the University of Oregon due to rampant pot smoking because there's really no way to spin that into anything other than what it is: a red flag.

The next step in the homestudy was a two-day infant-adoption training seminar, held over the course of a weekend at the agency's offices. We sat in the same mushroom-gray conference room where we'd met with the Angry Hippie. But this time, the lights were on and there were donuts and coffee. Besides us, there were five other couples, or, as Dave and I called them, the Competition. Most of them were considerably younger than us, late twenties or early thirties at best. One couple was in their sixties and had already raised four biological children. They wanted to spend their retirement years helping special-needs kids. We called them the Show-Offs.

The first day of the seminar was the usual seminar-y stuff. The agenda for the day read:

- Welcome
- Adoption Process
- Openness
- Grief and Loss
- Attachment and Bonding
- Cultural and Racial Identity Issues
- Post-Adoption Services
- Wrap-up

Most everything we covered that day was old news to me, having already studied all these issues in the Leaning Tower of Adoption Books that lived by my bed. The one new thing was the part where we got to talk to a real live birthmother, which happened toward the end of the first day. Until that point, we had only heard stories about birthmothers. To Dave and me, they were like mythic creatures who held enormous power over our lives. One of them would eventually choose us, sign the papers, and give us her child. The woman sitting before us nervously playing with her rings might as well have been a unicorn.

Angelika was in her mid-thirties, short and round, with dark curly hair and a kind of bubbly sarcasm that reminded me of Tony's sister Janice from *The Sopranos*. The daughter she'd placed for adoption at birth was now six years old. Her story included elements that would become very familiar to us over the next year: drug abuse, unprotected sex, abusive relationships, and a pregnancy that was greeted with ambivalence at best and panic at worst. She chose her daughter's adoptive parents because they were normal, stable, reliable. None of the things she felt she could ever be.

After she told us her story, we were given a chance to ask questions. An awkward silence followed, like it always does. Then we all flooded her with questions.

How often do you see your daughter now?

Once or twice a year.

How hard was it to give her up?

The hardest thing ever.

Do you regret it?

No. Not at all. But I still grieve.

What's your relationship with her?

I guess I'm kind of like an auntie.

Does she know who you are?

In her own way, yes. She knows that I carried her in my tummy. But her adoptive mom is her Mommy.

How do you feel about your daughter's adoptive parents?

I love them. They gave her everything I couldn't.

You don't resent them?

No. Sometimes I'm jealous of them. But I don't resent them.

Angelika hadn't planned the adoption beforehand. She'd been in denial about her pregnancy. She wasn't sure who the father was, didn't know how far along she might be. When labor came, she asked the nurse at the hospital to call an adoption agency. A case-worker brought her a stack of family books to look at, and from those she chose the couple that would be her daughter's parents. Hers was what was called an "instant baby," something we'd been told about earlier in the day. Instant babies don't happen that often, but they do happen, the agency told us.

"You never know with adoption," the woman running the seminar said. "You might just get a phone call in the middle of the night and then—*boom*—you're parents!"

I'm not sure if she thought she was being encouraging, but there wasn't a single person in the room who didn't turn pale when she said that.

Meeting Angelika went a long way toward easing our dis-comfort about open adoption. But not all the way. At least, not for me. Intellectually, open adoption made sense. But emotionally, it still didn't quite add up. It still felt like we would be sharing our child with someone else, even if that someone else was the person who had given that child life. It still felt like it would be confusing and stressful for everyone involved. It just didn't feel *right*. While I wanted to be as committed to the idea of open adoption as the people at the agency were (because I wanted to be that good, that selfless, that *open*), I just wasn't. I had reservations. Big ones. But three years had already passed. I didn't want to start over again, and I didn't have a Plan B. So I kept my mouth shut.

Dave, on the other hand, was on board. Being a pragmatist, he now saw a way for open adoption to work for us. In his mind, the whole thing was simply a matter of negotiation. We would meet with a birthmother and negotiate a level of openness that worked for everyone. And if we weren't able to reach an agreement, he and I would move on to the next birthmother. To him, the most important thing was brokering an adoption agreement that worked for us. No matter how long that took. To me, the most important thing was adopting a baby. Now. But, as I said, I kept my mouth shut.

The second day of the seminar was devoted to a single subject: substance abuse. We spent four hours learning about every possible drug a birthmother might take and the potential damage those drugs could cause to a child in the short and long term. We talked about pot, meth, crack, heroin, cocaine, prescription pills, cigarettes, and alcohol. While other expectant parents all over the city were attending childbirth classes, we listened to strange equations and comparisons like, "A crack baby is much better off than a meth baby." Or, "Heroin is actually better for the baby than methadone."

Then we took a break and decorated onesies with puff paint.

What the fuck?

Dave and I had spent so many years mired in an increasingly difficult struggle to get pregnant. By the time we left that world, we understood it. We spoke the language. We knew our way around. Now we were on a completely different planet, one whose terrain we could barely recognize. One that was populated primarily by women who couldn't have children and women who couldn't stop having children. By women who would have given anything to be pregnant and pregnant women who couldn't give a shit about the baby they were carrying.

Now, was that a gross generalization? Of course it was. Do I know better now? Yes, I do. But then, on that day, hearing about meth babies and crack babies and fetal alcohol syndrome, I was angry. Because I was setting myself up to be judged by women whose lives were out of control in ways I couldn't even fathom. Because I was expected to be okay with the idea of letting a drug addict into my life for the rest of my life. Because I had done everything right and yet I was the one who had to answer 120 questions and fork over $25,000. Because they had done everything wrong and yet they had absolute control over my future. And then, after coming to understand all of this over the course of two days, I was supposed to switch gears and decorate a fucking onesie? With puff paint? What planet was I on?

After the seminar came the actual home visit by a clinician from the agency. Thankfully, we hadn't been assigned to the Angry Hippie, but to a young woman named Cindy who was in her late twenties and appeared to possess a functioning sense of humor.

"Hi! I'm Cindy, and I'm here to judge you," she said as she stood smiling on our front porch.

We liked Cindy.

"What a great house," she said as she took off her coat. "I've always loved the Craftsman style."

She looked around the living room.

"And Kentucky Fried Chicken."

She was referring to the life-size statue of Colonel Sanders that was the focal point of our living room. His previous home was in the lobby of the ad agency. Dave had used his position as partner to justify an obsessive and sometimes disturbing collection of advertising figures, from the Colonel to Speedy Alka-Seltzer to Aunt Jemima. All of them came home with us when the agency folded.

"We used to have the Jolly Green Giant, too. But we sold him to some guy in California," I offered. "I had to give him a sponge bath before we shipped him off."

What was I doing? Why was I speaking?

"Let's get started," Cindy said, choosing to take the high road and ignore the unraveling freak show that was standing before her. "Why don't you give me a tour?"

We went into the dining room, which housed my extensive collection of vintage cocktail shakers and general cocktail memorabilia. Plus a Prohibition-era hideaway bar filled with enough liquor to open my own speakeasy.

I probably should have put those away.

"You'll want to put those bottles up on a high shelf," Cindy said, unfazed by my obvious alcoholism.

She stopped to look inside the Heywood-Wakefield cabinet, which housed one of my more esoteric collections.

"What are these guys?" she asked.

"Food with faces," I said. "I collect them."

"Umm, why?" she asked.

It was a fair question.

"I just like the idea of anthropomorphic food," I said. "My favorites are the ones that look like they used to be human but were turned into food by some kind of magic spell and now they're just trying to become human again."

Cindy pulled out a set of salt and pepper shakers that had human bodies and banana heads.

"Like these?" she asked.

"Exactly! See how unhappy they are? They have bananas for heads."

"Who would want that?"

"No one," I said emphatically. "No one would want that."

"How come the garlic guys are all cranky-looking?" she asked.

We were going to be friends. I could tell.

"Because they smell bad," I said. "And their heads are made of garlic."

"This is the weirdest conversation I've ever had," she said, sounding more than a little impressed.

"Do you want to see my Japanese vinyl collection?" Dave asked.

"He means action figures," I told Cindy. The alarmed look on her face told me she was picturing something else.

"Maybe later. Where does this door go?" Cindy had her hand on the door that led from the kitchen to the basement stairs.

"Nowhere," Dave and I said at the same time.

"I mean, it's just the basement," Dave said. "Nothing interesting down there."

"Right, but I'll need to see it anyway," Cindy said, turning the knob.

No. Oh, no.

I am a compulsively neat person. And even though our house is filled with stuff, people often remark that it doesn't look or feel cluttered. That's because I have a pathological need to have every single thing in its place. For as long as anyone can remember, I've been like this. The dark side of being a neatnik is that you need a place to put the things you don't know what to do with. You need a place for the things that don't have a place. You also need a place to put all of your husband's ugly shit that he lugs home from flea markets and garage sales, thinking he's going to use them for a Halloween prop someday but never does. Many of these things are disturbing. Many of them used to be living animals. All of them are in our basement, the door to which was now wide open.

"But our child will never go down there!" I called to Cindy, who was halfway down the basement stairs.

"That's okay," she called back. "I need to see it anyway."

Dave looked at me and shrugged his shoulders. He followed her down the stairs while I stood in the kitchen with my face buried in my hands. For the next twenty minutes, I paced the black-and-white checkerboard floor, convinced that by showing Cindy the contents of our basement, we had just slammed the door on any possibility of becoming adoptive parents. Because no one gives a baby to people who fuse an owl's head onto a bobcat's body. They just don't.

When she and Dave came back up, they were both laughing like old friends.

"Show me that iguana," Cindy said to Dave as she helped herself to a glass of water.

I caught Dave's eye and raised an eyebrow, silently asking *What the fuck happened down there?* He shrugged his shoulders yet again and said, "We need to install a handrail in the stairway."

When I was little, and the TV show *Candid Camera* was popular, I became obsessed with the idea that I was secretly being filmed. I lived in constant fear that every embarrassing moment of my life would be broadcast on television and the entire third grade would know that I pretended my pillow was Shaun Cassidy. To cope with this fear, I developed a habit of scanning every room for hidden cameras. That's what I was doing as I led a smiling and apparently unconcerned Cindy to the Dump Room. Because there was just no way I wasn't being set up.

The Dump Room was no longer filled with boxes and boxes of crap (those had moved to the basement, naturally), but it did still have a smelly, old iguana in it. And it was in no way ready to house a baby.

"This is great," said Cindy. "It'll be so cozy."

"You're not concerned about the iguana?" I asked, determined to appear to be the reasonable one once the footage was released.

"No. Dave told me he'd be moving down to the basement eventually."

"Right. The basement. The one you just saw and *didn't* emerge screaming from."

"Oh, it's not that bad," she said, waving her hand to dismiss my concerns. Kind of like George W. Bush did when he saw New Orleans after Hurricane Katrina.

And yet, despite my fear that we would not only be rejected but also possibly arrested, we passed the home inspection. The only thing left to do, Cindy reminded us before she left, was the family book.

The family book. Otherwise known as The Parent Catalog. This was the album each prospective parent had to put together. It was supposed to show a birthmother who we are, what we believe in, and what kind of parents we were going to be. The birthparents look through stacks of these books in search of the people they will ultimately give their child to. That's an awful lot of pressure to put on an eight-and-a-half-by-eleven loose-leaf binder. In fact, the very prospect of trying to capture such profoundly intangible qualities through a few pictures and paragraphs is enough to terrify most people. But Dave and I are not most people.

We work in advertising.

Our family book begins, as all family books do, with a "Dear Birthparent" letter from each of us. (Really. They make you do that.) In terms of difficulty, writing this letter was second only to writing my father's eulogy. Here's what mine said:

Dear Birthparent,

Could there be a more impersonal way to start such a personal letter? I have no idea who you are, yet this letter to you is one of the most important things I'll ever write. If I think about that too much, it might drive me crazy. So I guess I'll just dive in.

I want to start by saying that I cannot imagine what you're going through. I'll never know what it's like to be pregnant, or to give birth, or to make an unbelievably hard decision like the one you're about to make. Even so, I have a huge amount of respect for what you're doing.

What can I tell you about us? My husband Dave and I have been married for a little over four years, but we've been together for twelve. We took a long time before deciding to get married because we wanted to make sure that it would be forever. For the last six years, we've lived in a nearly hundred-year-old Craftsman bungalow with a big front porch. On the inside are all the weird, cool collections we've built together over the years. On the outside is a gorgeous garden that Dave created practically from scratch. We live in a great neighborhood with a really good school district and lots of friends close by.

We're both from big families. Dave is the oldest of four, with three younger sisters who are all as hilarious as he is. His mom and dad are nuts, but in a good way. And his cousins are all treated like siblings. Most of his family lives in Southern California, but we visit them often.

I'm the youngest of five and I have four nephews and two nieces, some of whom already have their own kids. Most of my family is here in Oregon, so we see them a lot. My sister and I are particularly close, and she's really looking forward to being an auntie again.

What else? Dave and I are both creative people who are lucky enough to be able to work at home, and we built a home office in our basement. Dave also combines his artistic talent with his love of Halloween to create a haunted house every year.

I know Dave is writing his own letter to you, but let me tell you a little bit about him from my point of view. Dave has always known that he wanted a child, and I can't wait to see him as a father. He's sweet and gentle and patient. Kids love him for all those reasons, but also because he's goofy and funny—basically a giant kid himself. One of our friends' kids refers to him as "Crazy Dave." He's going to be an amazing dad.

We tried to get pregnant for a little over two years. We didn't exhaust our options—there were still things we could have tried. But we both felt very strongly about adoption, and at a certain point, we felt like we were being pointed in that direction by forces that are bigger than us. I'm not a religious person, but I do believe in God and in fate. And I believe that adoption is the path we're supposed to take. There is a baby out there that is meant to be with us. And when the time is right, it will happen.

If we're the couple you eventually choose, saying "Thank you" seems ridiculously insufficient. In fact, if I said "Thank you" a million times, it still wouldn't be enough. Just know that if you do choose us, we will cherish your baby every day for the rest of our lives, and beyond. It will be the most important thing we'll ever do.

Again, I can't even begin to imagine the decision you have in front of you. But I admire you for making it. Even if I don't know you, and even if you don't choose us.

Many thanks,

Stacy

And here's what Dave wrote:

Dear Birthparent,

This is one of those times that I'm thankful my wife is a writer. Stacy covered a lot of the bases there and gave you a good indication of our background, life, and beliefs. So I think it's safe to use my letter to share a personal story with you.

My best friend once asked me to raise his children if anything were to happen to him. My first reaction was to reassure him that he wasn't going to die in a plane crash, and the chances of him being eaten by dingoes were slim to none. But as it turned out, he was as serious as he could be. I asked him why me—especially since he had three brothers, all of whom were fathers, not to mention his own parents to rely on. Plus, there was his ex-wife and all of her family.

He told me that he thought I would do a better job of making sure his kids grew up to be good, well-rounded, educated, and interesting people than anyone else he'd ever met, and that he knew there was nothing I wouldn't do for those kids. With the possible exception of Stacy agreeing to spend the rest of her life with me, I think this was probably the single greatest compliment that anyone's ever paid me. That anyone could pay me, really. After all, he was talking about entrusting me with his own flesh and blood. So I thanked him for his trust and told him I'd be honored, and that he had nothing to worry about. I would love and care for his son and daughter as if they had always been my own.

And as I was thinking about this letter, it occurred to me that that is exactly what I'm saying to you now. I know it sounds high-handed, but Stacy and I are both truly honored that you would consider us as adoptive parents, and that this is a trust we are going to honor forever.

As I was growing up, I always envisioned myself as a father. When we found out we were unable to have children, oddly enough, I wasn't heartbroken. Maybe crestfallen is a better word. Sure, it was a blow, but I never saw it as the end of the line. I've always thought of adoption as not only a viable option but a socially responsible one as well. I know that someday, Stacy and I will share the home we've created with someone who needs that home, and that our family will be as real as anyone else's.

If that someone is your child, you have my thanks. For your openness and your generosity, for your consideration and your responsibility, for your selflessness and your trust. Stacy and I both promise to be worthy of that trust. And it's my pleasure to make to you the same promise I made to my best and oldest friend.

Thank you,

Dave

The rest of the book consisted of a carefully curated and tastefully arranged series of photos of me and Dave and our friends and family, accompanied by witty captions designed to communicate exactly how awesome we are.

And it worked.

One week after submitting the book to the agency, we were chosen by a young couple. They were expecting a girl. And they were expecting her in two weeks.

CHAPTER THIRTEEN

The Chosen Ones

Panic does not even begin to cover it. When Dave and I got off the phone with Cindy, we spent a minute or two being silently flabbergasted before the Great Freak-Out of 2006 began. I was the first one to break the silence. The first word out of my mouth after being told that we were going to be parents in less than two weeks?

Iguana.

"You're outta here, big guy," I said, standing in the middle of the near-nursery after sprinting up there from the basement office where we'd taken the call. I was bending over and staring at Elvis, who was bobbing his head up and down. This behavior, Dave had told me, was territorial. It was Elvis's way of saying, "I was here first."

"Suck it, Godzilla. Your days are numbered."

"Calm down," Dave said. He was out of breath after running up the stairs after me. "Do not panic."

"Why on earth not?" I asked.

"Because it doesn't help anything."

"That's not true," I said. "It makes me feel like I'm accomplishing something."

"That's retarded," Dave said.

I know you are, but what am I?

"We're not ready for this," I said.

"So maybe we should pass," he said, leaning against the door frame.

"Pass? On the baby?"

"Yeah."

"ARE YOU FUCKING INSANE?"

"Look, we were told to expect a six-month wait. It's only been a week. And like you said, we're not ready. Maybe we should—"

"We are not passing on this baby, Dave. We've been trying to become parents for two years. I had my insides vacuumed out so that we could become parents. When I say we're not ready, that doesn't mean we pass. That means we need to *get* ready."

Tears were welling up in my eyes. I willed myself not to cry.

"I'm just playing devil's advocate," he said, maddeningly calm.

"Right. I know. You love to do that," I said. "But the thing about the devil's advocate is, it sucks being married to him."

"Don't get defensive. I'm just—"

"We are not talking about buying a car, Dave. We're talking about a baby. Somewhere in Portland, there's a pregnant woman who looked at our book and said, 'I want to give them my baby.' That's the most difficult decision she's probably ever had to make. And we're not going to tell her no just because you can't get off your ass and find a new home for your fucking iguana!"

He was quiet for a moment, but there was anger in his eyes. When he finally spoke, his voice was cold and measured.

"What do we need?" he said.

"Everything. A crib. A changing table. Clothes. Car seat. Everything," I said.

"Okay, that's what baby showers are for. Call the Coven and tell them to throw us a shower. What else?"

"Elvis."

"Fine. I'll take care of it," he said, and stomped off.

I got in my car and drove to Babies"R"Us.

—◆—

"I can't breathe," I said into the phone.

I was sitting in my car with the air-conditioning working overtime to beat back the July heat. The sweat that had dampened my bangs and pasted them to my forehead was finally evaporating.

My friend Pat was on the other line.

"Why didn't you call me, sweetie?" she asked. "You don't go in there alone. That's a rookie move."

"But I need stuff. I don't have any stuff."

"In through the nose, out through the mouth, babe. Let me hear you do it."

I complied.

"Good. Okay, here's the thing: You don't need that much stuff right away. Just a couple of things."

"She doesn't have anywhere to sleep!" I yelled, the panic rising back up in my chest like a bubble.

"I still have Nora's bassinet. You can have it," Pat said.

"Car seat! I don't have a car seat. I tried to go in there and buy one, but that place? It's horrible, Pat. I don't belong in there."

"I know. That's why you never go alone. Especially your first time. We'll go get you a car seat tomorrow. I'll go with you."

"What if she's born tonight?"

"She's not going to be born tonight."

"BUT WHAT IF SHE IS?"

"Then we'll still go get one tomorrow. You're not taking a baby home two hours after she's born," Pat said. "It doesn't work that way."

Pat has two kids. She knows things.

"Oh my God. I already suck at this! What am I doing?"

"Go home, Stacy. Turn your car around and go home. Make yourself a gin and tonic. Then go to bed."

"Okay," I said, my eyes following a young couple loading their SUV with diapers.

"You're going to be fine," Pat said, unconvincingly.

"I don't have any diapers."

"Go. Home."

I backed the car out slowly. It would be just my luck to hit a pregnant woman in the parking lot of Babies"R"Us. That would really tie a bow on the whole experience.

Near the entrance to the store, there are a bunch of parking spots marked reserved for expectant mommies. Instead of a wheelchair, there's a silhouette of a stork on the sign. Even though I was, technically, expecting a baby any minute, I didn't park in one of those spots. They weren't for people like me. It would be like parking in a handicapped spot when you're just really neurotic. The remainder of my brief visit to Babies"R"Us was colored with the same crayon: the you-don't-belong-here crayon. It's kind of a pukey green with a subtle undertone of bile.

As I left the parking lot and headed for the freeway, I punched the gas a little too hard and heard the tires of my gray Beetle squeal. As the store's grammatically offensive neon sign got smaller and smaller behind me, I turned up the radio: *Mommy's all right. Daddy's all right. They just seem a little weird . . .*

The birthmother's name was Jordan. We didn't know very much about her, other than the fact that she was twenty-two and didn't want any contact after the placement. Despite talking the talk about open adoption, Dave and I did a happy dance when we learned that Jordan was willing to hand us her baby and walk off into the sunset. I was also thrilled that she was having a girl. I knew I didn't have the right to be picky at this point, but I'd always wanted a girl. Or, more accurately, I'd never wanted a boy. Boys can go wrong. Really wrong. But a girl was something I understood.

Which was good, because I was about to become a mother to one. And I needed stuff.

A baby shower was the obvious solution, but it seemed wrong to me. As with the special parking spots at Babies"R"Us, I didn't feel like I had a right to one. Baby showers are for pregnant women. But the Coven, once they got wind of this, would have none of it. In less time than it took me to decide which car seat to register for, they had invited all of our friends to our house for what would turn out to be the world's drunkest baby shower.

Pat, Marie, and Courtenay did all the work, including developing a series of theme drinks for the occasion. There was the Rosemary's Baby, a martini with rosemary-infused gin and a tiny plastic baby as garnish. There was the Nighty-Night, a pinkish punch containing at least three different kinds of alcohol. And there was the Dip-Tet, which was really just a tequila shot followed by a Hello Kitty bandage. By the end of the night, there was hardly anyone who had less than two bandages on their arm. I had five.

The next morning, as I stumbled out of bed, throbbing and dehydrated, I saw that my living room had been obliterated by the eruption of Mount Baby Stuff. Our friends had supplied us with a car seat, a stroller, clothes, shoes, a bathtub, a changing pad, a diaper bag, bottles, sippy cups, a humidifier, a full set of bedding, and an infant first-aid kit featuring itty-bitty tweezers. Our parents bought us the crib and changing table. My biggest client gifted me with eight hundred diapers. We had everything we needed.

Just in time for Jordan to change her mind.

CHAPTER FOURTEEN

Alarms, False and Otherwise

"I just don't think she was ever serious about adoption," Cindy was telling us over the phone. "She wanted her boyfriend to commit to raising the baby with her, and now he's agreed."

"So that's that?" I asked.

"Pretty much," she said. "The boyfriend told me he wanted to see how it goes, and if it's not working out, they'd revisit adoption in a few months."

"*If it's not working out?* Like it's a dog they take back to the pound? Can they really do that?"

"It won't happen. Trust me," Cindy said. "If it's not working out in a few months, he'll just leave. Jordan has no intention of placing her baby for adoption. I'm really sorry, but this kind of thing does happen sometimes."

"But we just had a baby shower," I said, wondering if I now had to return all those gifts.

"That's great! Now you're that much more ready for when it really happens," Cindy chirped.

That answers that.

"I don't know whether to feel sad or relieved," I told Dave after hanging up the phone.

"I think a little bit of both is in bounds," he said.

And he was right. On the one hand, we weren't emotionally ready for that baby. There's a very good reason human babies gestate for nine months. A person needs some space between pregnancy and birth to get used to the idea. And even though Dave and I had been trying to become parents for more than three years by this point, that didn't mean we were prepared to become parents in an instant. We needed some space to get used to the idea. Now that Jordan had changed her mind, we'd be able to have it.

On the other hand, we had come remarkably close to being done with the whole maddening, interminable process of trying and trying and trying to become parents. Once again, we found ourselves starting over at square one. Once again, we had to tell our friends and families that it just hadn't worked out this time. Once again, we had to wait.

Fortunately, we had plenty of things to keep us occupied. I had a busy roster of freelance clients to attend to, plus a nursery to decorate. Dave still had an iguana cage to build, but not before moving the haunted house to a bigger location. His relationship with the owner of the haunt at the Jantzen Beach mall had deteriorated.

There can only be one Alpha Nerd, and Dave has never been one to back down, so in March of that year, he was asked to leave. By April, Dave had an offer to set up his own haunt at Portland's Memorial Coliseum in October. The attraction would be called Fright Town and would feature three separate haunts, all of which would be created and produced by Dave. Once we got the news that the baby wasn't going to happen, he dove headfirst into haunt prep and didn't look back. That left me alone to brood about the nursery, the someday baby, and my cat Nancy, whose health was failing despite my attempts to deny it.

Nancy had been with me since the day she was born, twenty years earlier. I was a silly, irresponsible college student who had jumped in my 1977 Datsun and moved home for the summer, bringing with me nothing but my clothes and a pregnant stray cat who gave birth to a litter of three on Father's Day. I had spent the previous night in Eugene, cleaning out my old apartment. When I pulled into my parents' driveway that morning, my dad was waiting for me.

"Congratulations," he said, drying his hands with a dishtowel. "You're a grandmother."

We eventually gave away two of the kittens (including her brother, Sid), and my parents agreed to keep the mama, but Nancy was mine. Or rather, I was hers. From the time she was old enough to climb up on the bed, she would wake me every morning with a gentle paw to the face. When I opened my eyes, there she'd be, jet black except for her white chin and feet, staring at me with the most intent look I'd ever seen. While the other kittens were off raising hell, Nancy was always with me, patiently waiting for me to give her my attention. When it didn't come soon enough for her liking, Nancy would lay her paw on my arm and say *Oww?*

So she stayed with me through college and apartments and jobs and boyfriends. She endured the addition of interlopers like Zooey, Chopper, and Dave. She got comically fat and had bad teeth that needed expensive attention. When she was fifteen, Nancy was diagnosed with thyroid cancer, which had been manageable with a daily pill. Until now. Around the time we were finishing up the homestudy, she'd become dehydrated and needed subcutaneous fluids administered every other day. That meant hanging a bag of saline from the curtain rod, placing Nancy on my lap, and holding her there while I inserted a huge needle under her skin and let the fluids collect in an aqueous lump between her shoulder blades. The fact that she did not fight this should have told me all I needed to know.

One night in August, I was worried that she wasn't eating or drinking, so I took her to DoveLewis, an emergency animal hospital in Northwest Portland. It was one of the hottest nights of the year, and the waiting room was filled with heat-stroked dogs and cats. Nancy, usually very vocal in her disapproval of the vet, was quiet and still in her carrier. Once in a while she let out a quiet *Oww* and looked at me with those intent eyes.

It would be hours before they could see her, so I gathered up her carrier and brought her home. The next morning, I took her to her regular vet, who confirmed that her organs were shutting down and it was time for her to go.

"I'm so sorry, Nance," I said, breaking down in front of the same doctor who had put Zooey down two years earlier.

"This cat has lived for twenty years," Dr. Erickson said, stroking her fur. "You have nothing to be sorry for. You're doing right by her, just like you always have."

"You should be a shrink," I laughed, pawing at my tear-stained face.

"I like animals better," she said as she prepared the syringe.

Seconds after it went in, Nancy was gone. But not before leaving me with a parting gift: She emptied her bladder all over my shoes.

On my way out, one of the receptionists handed me a brochure on how to deal with the loss of a pet. When I flipped through it later that night, numbed by martinis and ice cream, I came across this quote: "Our pets shepherd us through certain eras of our lives. When we are ready to turn the corner and make it on our own, they let us go."

CHAPTER FIFTEEN

Sharp Corners

I got home late on a Tuesday night to see the message light blinking on our phone. I was helping out at Fright Town, which had opened the week before to sparse crowds. But now that Halloween was getting closer, attendance was picking up. Dave had gone out with some of the actors and volunteers, but I had an early meeting the next morning, so I came home. After listening to the message, I called his cell.

"We've been picked," I said to his voice mail. "Get your ass home."

Their names were Wendy and Josh. She was in her thirties and had two young kids from a previous marriage. He was in his twenties and had no desire to be a daddy. They weren't in a relationship anymore, but Josh was committed to seeing Wendy through the birth and adoption. She was due to deliver a boy in December.

On Wednesday, Dave and I went to the agency to meet with our new caseworker, Fran. After Jordan changed her mind, we were reassigned to Meg, the Angry Hippie. But she was on a sabbatical in India, so Fran was filling in. We liked her immediately. Fran was in her early sixties with gray bobbed hair and the kind of soft, buttery face that reminded me of someone's grandmother. (Not mine. Mine was mean.) She was the director of the infant-adoption program and didn't handle cases anymore, but she was making an exception because they were understaffed.

We sat in Fran's beige office and got to know each other while we waited for Sharon, who was Wendy and Josh's caseworker. It's agency policy that adoptive parents and birthparents have separate caseworkers so there's no bias toward one side or the other.

"Hi! I'm Sharon!" she said as she shoved the door open with her shoulder. She was sturdy and blonde, lugging a giant purple handbag, a battered briefcase spilling over with files, and the largest iced coffee I had ever seen.

"I already feel like I know you guys, what with the Jordan thing and all," she said, dumping her bags on the round conference table and taking a long pull of her iced coffee. "I'm so sorry you guys got caught up in that, by the way. What a mess! *Eughhh!*"

That last word was more of a gesture, with Sharon waving her hands near her face and shaking her head vigorously. She reminded me of Joanne Worley. She blew her bangs out of her eyes and sat down at the table with us. We each shook her hand and agreed, telepathically, that we would forever refer to her as Hurricane Sharon.

"So let me start by saying congratulations on being chosen," Fran said.

"Yes! Congratulations!" said Sharon. "Although no one here was surprised. As soon as we saw your family book, we all knew you guys were going to get picked right away."

"And we did," said Dave. "Twice."

"Yes," Fran said. "And again, we are sorry that happened. But that's one of the realities of adoption."

"We know," I said, not wanting to start off with a confrontation. "And it was really for the best, because we weren't ready for that baby."

"Well, you'll have some time to get ready for this one," Fran said. "What questions can we answer for you about Wendy and Josh?"

"Do they want to meet us?" I asked.

"Yes, very much," Fran said. "They're eager to get to know you two."

"How soon can we meet?"

"Let's see . . . We have a few approved dates to choose from," Fran said, flipping through a file on her desk.

"Approved dates?" Dave asked. "Approved by whom?"

"Her parole officer," Sharon said, ever so matter-of-factly.

"Wendy is under house arrest for identity theft," Fran said, in quick response to our raised eyebrows and dropped jaws.

"Uhhhhh . . ."

This was all Dave could think to say. Which is a syllable more than I was able to muster.

"Let's back up a bit and give you the whole picture," Fran said.

Wendy, as it turns out, had been arrested for identity theft earlier in the year and was placed under house arrest when she found out she was pregnant. She lost custody of her son and daughter as a result of the conviction. It was unclear whether she was going to get custody back, but Sharon thought that putting her baby up for adoption might make Wendy's ex more willing to let her have the kids back. It was, after all, a very responsible decision.

And she might have used meth once or twice. But not when she was pregnant.

Probably.

"So wouldn't that count as duress?" I asked, ignoring the meth issue and focusing on her ex telling her she had to give up her baby in order to get her other kids back.

According to Oregon law, if a birthmother can prove she was under duress when she signed the papers, the adoption can be invalidated. Same goes for fraud. But those are the only two ways a birthparent can take back a child.

"We wouldn't be talking to you if we thought so," Sharon said. "I've spent a lot of time with Wendy and Josh, and I think they're doing this because they want to. Because they believe it's the best thing for their son. Besides, her ex-husband has no legal grounds to make that claim."

"Okay. So what's the next step?" I asked.

"We all sit down together," Fran said.

"So you'll be with us when we meet with them?" Dave asked.

"Yes. Both Sharon and I will be there to help guide the discussion. We'll meet here at the offices." She looked back at the file on her desk. "The first available date is November first."

The day after Halloween.

"We'll take it," I said, before Dave had a chance to object. He would be exhausted, of course. But I didn't want to waste any time. Two weeks was bad enough.

Driving home, I knew Dave's head was filling up with doubts about Wendy. But I also knew he was keeping his mouth shut for my sake. And I was perfectly willing to let him.

For the next two weeks Dave had the haunt to keep him occupied. Which left me to go quietly insane all by myself. After all this time, you'd think I would have gotten better at waiting, but it still made me want to punch a wall. My sister-in-law was pregnant again, due in January. So was my friend Kelly. I desperately wanted to believe that by the time their babies were born, I would be a mother.

I passed the time by obsessing over the upcoming meeting with the birthparents and harassing LeeAnne.

From: Stacy Bolt
Sent: Wednesday, October 25, 2006 1:14 PM PDT
To: LeeAnne Miller
Subject: Need Adoption Advice!

Hi lady,

Help! I need your advice. We're meeting with a potential birthmom next Wednesday, and I'm scared shitless! Did you meet with JJ and Annie's birthparents? What was it like?

Thanks!
Stacy

From: LeeAnne Miller
Sent: October 25, 2006 1:35:04 PM PDT
To: Stacy Bolt
Subject: RE: Need Adoption Advice!

Stacy,

Yep, we met with JJ's b-parents, and it was bizarre but cool to see a preview of what our kid might look like. It's very odd to see this very pregnant woman and know that it might be YOUR kid she's carrying. You just have to kind of remain detached a bit and go with the flow . . . if it is meant to be, then it will be . . .

You need to be really clear on your boundaries as far as openness. Don't be afraid to say "This is how we see our relationship with you," and lay it out for her. I would imagine that you would be fine with consistent updates sent through the agency (so no identifying info on your end) that she can share with the half-siblings if she feels that need. You might even feel comfortable meeting with her in a public place periodically. She was probably into meth, is that right? Seems like often those people have grandiose ideas but no follow-through, so she might say she wants a lot of openness, but will you even be able to find her down the road? That's why it's a good idea to use the agency as a go-between—it will be up to her to keep them updated with her contact info, and if they don't have it, they will file your updates and it doesn't become your problem to track her down . . .

Remember: This will be YOUR babe, and you, as momma, get to decide what is best. Don't agree to *anything* that doesn't sit well with you.

Write and tell me more ...
Hugs!
LeeAnne

Before talking to LeeAnne, I never thought of myself as having a right to ask anything of a birthmother. The fact that she would be giving me her child was so monumentally generous that making demands seemed almost crass. Beggars can't be choosers, right? I was so focused on the immediate, short-term goal of becoming a mother that I hadn't bothered to look beyond it. But the truth is, I *would* be this child's mother. I would feed him and change him and teach him. I would take care of him when he was sick and haul his ass out of a restaurant when he threw a tantrum. So I had rights.

This was a revelation to me.

CHAPTER SIXTEEN

Meet the Birthparents

The first of November was your average Oregon day: cold, cloudy, rainy. We'd gotten maybe three hours of sleep the night before— Dave, because he was out celebrating the end of Halloween season, and me, because I was up fretting all night. As we pulled into the agency parking lot, I was wound tight from a combination of nerves and an entire pot of coffee.

"Can I get you some coffee?" the receptionist asked us as we sat down to wait for Fran.

"No! Thank you. We're fine," Dave answered, knowing I would have said yes.

He flipped through that morning's paper while I considered throwing up. Before I could decide one way or the other, Fran appeared.

"Ready?" she asked, gesturing toward the hallway.

"Are they here yet?" I asked, throwing my purse over my shoulder.

"Yes. They're waiting for you," she said.

Definitely throwing up.

We followed Fran down the hall, past a series of cubicles where people sat doing their work. They acted as if nothing unusual was happening. As if the world wasn't about to change as soon as we walked through that door over there. But I guess people walked through that door all the time. Today it was our turn.

The first person I saw when I entered the room was Josh. He was young—so young—and thin, with a smattering of facial hair that looked like it had taken a long time to grow. He wore black jeans and a finely aged hoodie, work boots, and a trucker hat that said PLAYER on the front. He took it off when we walked in, revealing a mighty head of hat-hair.

"Hey, I'm Josh," he said eagerly, holding out his hand. "Good to meet you."

He smelled like stale cigarette smoke and didn't seem the least bit nervous.

I knew Wendy was behind me, sitting in the chair that was against the same wall as the door. But I was afraid to turn around. I was afraid of her.

"You changed your hair color," a woman's voice said from behind me.

I turned around to look at Wendy sitting in an overstuffed armchair, a box of Kleenex balancing on what lap she had left.

"I like it this way better," she said.

In the picture on the cover of our family book, my hair had been red—a momentary dalliance that hadn't suited me. On this morning it was back to its usual jet black.

"Do you think so?" I asked, tucking some strands behind my ear.

"For sure," Wendy said, smiling. "This brings out your eyes better. Hi." She held out her hand to me and I took it. We didn't so much shake hands as hold them, an electrical charge passing from one expectant mother to the next.

"I'd get up, but it might take a while," she said pointing at her belly.

It was huge, and she had a small frame, so it looked like she was being pinned down in the chair by a giant beach ball. A beach ball I could not stop staring at. Because that beach ball might be mine.

Wendy had shoulder-length dark hair, ruddy skin, and brown eyes. She wore a pink button-up cotton shirt and black pants. The legs rode up just enough to reveal the electronic monitoring brace-let around her ankle, its green light blinking steadily. Although her voice and demeanor were soft and kind, her face had a hard edge to it. She reminded me of the girls in high school who smoked in the parking lot and threatened to beat you up in the bathroom after Spanish. Those girls always went with boys like Josh.

For the next few minutes, all six of us sat down and engaged in the most awkward small talk of all time. How about the weather? Big plans for Thanksgiving? Anybody watch the Blazers game last night?

SERIOUSLY? There is a pregnant woman RIGHT OVER THERE and she's thinking about giving us her baby. HER BABY! Is this really the time to talk about our shitty basketball team?

I know Fran and Sharon were just trying to ease us into the meeting. But that didn't make it any less annoying or awkward.

Reality set in when Wendy started sobbing uncontrollably.

"I'm sorry," she said, wiping her nose on the back of her hand. "I do this all the time. Hormones, you know?"

Nope. I don't.

"It's just that I've been so worried about this meeting," she said. "I was worried that Stacy wouldn't like me and then they wouldn't want to adopt Logan. And I really, really want you guys to be his parents."

Wait. What?

"Wendy and Josh loved your book," Sharon added. "They knew right away that you were the ones."

Josh nodded solemnly while Wendy blew her nose.

"I just really want to know this is all going to work out," Wendy said, dabbing at her eyes to keep from smudging her makeup. "Once I know that, I feel like I can relax and get through the rest of the pregnancy."

"You were worried *we* wouldn't like *you?*" I asked, still struggling to piece together the situation.

LeeAnne had told me just the day before: "Remember—she's probably more scared of you than you are of her."

Like a bee, I thought. *Leave her alone and she won't sting you.*

"You call the baby Logan?" Dave asked. He had taken a seat next to Josh on the couch.

"Oh. Yeah," Wendy said. "That's just my name for him. You can name him whatever you want."

"It's not unusual for a birthmother to name the baby before she signs the papers," Fran explained gently. "Then the adoptive parents choose their own name. There will be two birth certificates."

Wendy started crying again.

I think this was the first time I really understood the reality of adoption: that one person's joy is predicated on another's pain.

"Wendy," I said, leaning forward to look her in the eye. "We are honored that you chose us. Of course we want to adopt your baby."

"Wonderful," said Fran, clapping her soft hands together. "Let's talk about visits then, shall we? Wendy, have you and Josh thought about how often you'd like to visit with the baby?"

"Once a week?" Wendy said in a tiny voice.

Long, deeply uncomfortable silence.

"Kidding. I'm kidding!" she said.

Relieved laughter all around.

"Stacy and Dave? How do you see this working?" Fran asked.

Don't be afraid to say "This is how we see our relationship with you," and lay it out for her.

"Umm, I don't know. I mean, I guess we'd be willing to work with Wendy and Josh on it," I said, already wanting to slap myself.

"Okay, then, once a week," Wendy said, smiling but not necessarily joking.

"The standard agreement is two visits a year plus pictures and updates once a month," Fran explained. "Dave and Stacy, is that something you'd feel comfortable with?"

"Definitely," Dave said.

I'd been benched for wussy-ness.

"Wendy and Josh, how about you?"

"Works for me," Josh said. He was dying to get out of the room.

"Umm, yeah. I guess so," Wendy said, her eyes welling up again. "Or maybe more than that? I was hoping for more than that."

"How about we meet again next week?" Sharon asked. "That'll give everyone some time to think about specifics, and we can hammer out an agreement."

We agreed to meet the following Wednesday, as long as Wendy's probation officer was okay with it. As we stood up to say our good-byes, Wendy looked at me and stretched her arms out. I walked over to her and let her pull me into an awkward embrace. She was a good two inches shorter than me, and I was wearing heels. So I bent my knees to get down to her level, and as I did, Wendy's huge stomach came to rest in the triangle between the tops of my legs and my stomach. It was as close as I had ever been to holding my own baby.

Wendy stood up on her tippy-toes and whispered in my ear, "Thank you."

Dave and I drove in silence for a while, the wipers working furiously against the Novemberness of the day. We crossed through downtown Portland, past Waterfront Park, and up the ramp to the Morrison Bridge, just in time to have the red-and-white safety gates come down in front of us. The drawbridge was going up. We'd have to wait a while.

Dave shut off the engine and stared out the window.

"So, what do you think?" he asked, still staring.

"I think we're going to be parents," I said.

He turned to look at me and smiled.

"I think you're right."

CHAPTER SEVENTEEN

Mandatory Waiting Period

Through a series of phone calls with Fran, a volley of e-mails, and two face-to-face meetings with Wendy and Josh, we finally came to an open-adoption agreement. For the first six months, Wendy and Josh would see the baby once a month. After that, we would revert to a standard schedule of two visits a year, plus pictures and updates once a month. Wendy had been adamant about seeing the baby regularly during the first few months of his life. "That's when they change the most," she'd said. Dave was deeply uncomfortable with the arrangement, but I kept remembering what LeeAnne had told me about "grandiose ideas but no follow-through." I was rolling the dice that Wendy would lose interest before the first six months were even up. Besides, I kept telling myself, he's going to be *our* baby.

All we had to do was wait.

Thanksgiving found us once again at Mark and Rachel's house. The twins were eighteen months old and, by all available evidence, in complete control of their parents' lives. What had once been a casually elegant home now looked like a teenager's bedroom. Discarded clothes in matching motifs hung from the edges of tables and chairs. Toys collected in the corners like dust bunnies. There was a thin sheen of what appeared to be a fruit glaze on everything. The parents, once buttoned-up professionals, were shells of their former selves. Rachel, always the very image of elegance, looked like she hadn't held a brush for over a week. And Mark, whose patrician features had always seemed Gatsbyesque, now had the haunted, empty quality of a Dorothea Lange Dust Bowl portrait.

If my sister Julie and I hadn't jumped in and taken control of dinner, we might have all died from trichinosis. As it was, dinner was spent like a tennis match, with the guests' heads swiveling left and right to Rachel and Maya on one end of the table, and Mark and Michael on the other. They had begun to snipe at each other's parenting skills, completely oblivious to the fact that there were four guests seated at their table, or that it was Thanksgiving, or that there was a world that existed beyond their two toddlers and the Brazilian au pair who appeared to be no help at all.

"Mark, did you remember to heat up the peach puree?"

"No. Was I supposed to?"

"It's the only thing Maya will eat, Mark. You know that."

"She's eighteen months old, Rachel. She should be eating something other than peach puree."

"So I'm a bad mother. Is that what you're saying?"

To be fair, they both kind of sucked. And it was a pretty big letdown, frankly. Mark and Rachel had been our shining beacons of hope. They had become parents after years of trying. They had stuck with it and made it work despite the devastating setbacks. And now they were being brought down by peach puree.

On the drive home, Dave and I never actually said it out loud, but the implication was clear: We would never be like that.

The day after Thanksgiving, Julie and I hosted Slayerfest, our annual tradition in which we and several friends sit around in our sweats and watch a dozen or so episodes of *Buffy the Vampire Slayer*, a show we both believe to be the greatest in the history of television. While this was happening, Dave was under strict orders to begin construction of Iguana House 2.0, a bigger, better version of Elvis's cage to be located in our basement office. For weeks, the nursery had been slowly coming to life, with the crib set up on one end and the closet filled with tiny clothes on tiny hangers. It was perfect, as long as you didn't turn around and see the crotchety old reptile on the other end.

When I returned from Slayerfest later that evening, full of junk food and wine, my head nearly came off. Our living room was filled with particle board and chicken wire and Plexiglas panels, but nothing had been assembled. Dave was in the other room watching *Dr. Who*.

"Hi, honey," I said through my teeth. "Why the fuck isn't Elvis's cage being built?"

"It's going to take more than a day," he said, on the defensive.

"Yes, but it appears that you haven't even started. Sweetie."

I threw in that last part to show him that I still loved him even though I was thinking about how to make his death look like an accident.

"I need some more stuff. I can't get started without this other . . . stuff."

To be fair, he probably used an actual building term here, but time and my righteous fury have erased the name of it.

"Okay. So why didn't you get this *stuff*?" I asked.

"Everything's closed. It's a holiday," he said, the condescension dripping from his tongue and rolling down his chin.

No jury in the world would convict me.

"Dave. It's the day after Thanksgiving. Every store in the history of stores is open until midnight. So please. Darling. Get off your ass, go to the fucking store, and get your goddamned stuff."

This exchange, I told myself, was good. Healthy, even. It was preparing me for how to deal with our son when he was a sullen, stupid teenager.

While Dave was out getting stuff, I called our friends Roland and Amy. They lived two blocks away and were the very best kind of people: the kind who are always willing to help you do hard things. They showed up the next morning, Roland with a toolbox and Amy with a stack of magazines. The menfolk would build things with stuff while the womenfolk pored over design magazines in search of the perfect nursery decor. We also polished off a bottle of wine and put together a huge pot of chili.

By the time the long holiday weekend was over, Iguana House 2.0 was fully operational, and the iguana in question had been removed from the nursery and installed in his new digs. A mere two years after I'd first asked Dave to do it.

Finally free to decorate at will, I decorated at will. I filled shelves with books and stuffed animals. I hung tiny clothes on tiny hangers. I bought diapers and wipes and butt cream and put them all in coordinating baskets underneath the changing table. The final touch was a vintage crib mobile I'd bought at an antique show the summer after we'd quit trying to get pregnant. It was the first thing I'd ever allowed myself to buy for the baby we thought we might never have.

Once we had made the decision to adopt, we had a new sense of optimism. We'd let go of all the uncertainty and superstition that had hung over us while we were trying to conceive and were finally able to focus on a single truth: We were going to have a baby. So when I saw that painted wooden crib mobile with pink and blue birds circling around each other, I just bought it. No cautionary thoughts about hubris this time. I bought it for the baby we were going to have. And as I walked away from the booth, Dave and I held hands like the expectant parents we were.

We had one more meeting with Wendy and Josh in early December. When Dave and I walked into the now-familiar meeting room, Wendy handed me a black-and-white photograph.

"I thought you'd like to have a picture of your son," she said.

I looked down at the photo. It was a sonogram.

"Got that one yesterday," she said. "Everything's perfect."

I was honestly too stunned to speak. Until that moment, the baby Wendy was carrying was just that: the baby Wendy was carrying. But now, it was my son. She'd said so. And I could see him. Now I was the one who was crying.

Wendy reached over and rubbed my back. "I'm so glad you're going to be his mom," she whispered.

Once I'd pulled myself together, the subject at hand was delivery day. Specifically, we needed to talk to Wendy and Josh about how they wanted things to happen at the hospital.

"How does it usually work?" Wendy asked Hurricane Sharon.

"It all depends on what you want," she said. "I've seen some people invite the adoptive parents into the delivery room for the birth. Other people want to have that time for themselves. It just depends on what you want, Wendy."

"I don't think I want that. To have you guys in the delivery room," Wendy said in a small voice. "Sorry."

"That's totally fine," I said, putting my hand on hers. And it was. I had no designs on witnessing the birth. That was something I'd let go of when we'd stopped trying to get pregnant. Besides, it would just be weird. This wasn't our moment; it was Wendy and Josh's. And the baby wouldn't be ours until they signed the papers the next day. Being present at the birth seemed almost ghoulish. *Hi! We're here to take your baby away!*

In the end, we agreed to wait and see what Wendy wanted when the time came. If she wanted us to be in the waiting room, we would. If she wanted us to wait until the next day when the papers were ready, we'd do that. This wasn't our game, and we didn't get to call it. So we went home, tacked the sonogram up on the refrigerator, and started decorating for Christmas.

Halloween is Dave's holiday. Christmas is mine. I have a massive collection of vintage Christmas decorations and ornaments, some of which are actual family heirlooms but most gathered over years of trawling flea markets and dusty antiques shops. In order to properly display all of my holiday treasures, most of our regular treasures have to be displaced for the season. Decorating for Christmas is a big, fat deal. And I, being the peacock that I am, cannot be content with just looking at the collection myself. I need everyone else to look at it, too. So I host a cocktail party every year, modeled directly after the ones my parents used to have in the '70s. Everyone gets dressed up, fancy canapés are served, swinging music is swung to, and all the grown-ups are completely shitfaced. I couldn't wait for our child to be older, so he could weave in and out of the dancing, laughing crowd like I used to, secure in the knowledge that he can get away with pretty much anything while the grown-ups are otherwise occupied.

This year, the decorations went up as usual, but the party was canceled. We had a baby to get ready for, and there was just no way I could pull off a cocktail party in my current state of anxiety. Also canceled was our trip to Southern California to spend Christmas with Dave's family. We went every other year, but since the baby was due on the twenty-second, we canceled the tickets we'd bought in September and hunkered down to get ready for Jack.

Dave and I had gone around and around on names, but we eventually settled on Jackson Cash Helfrey. The Jackson part passed Dave's Supreme Court justice test, as in "Supreme Court justice Jackson Helfrey today ruled that alcohol is unconstitutional." But the shortened version also passed my Rat Pack test, as in, could a person with that name have once been a member of the Rat Pack? Jack Helfrey. Ring-a-ding-ding. And the Cash part? We just liked it. We're both big Johnny Cash fans, and there was just something cool about sticking it in the middle, almost like a hidden surprise.

Jackson Cash Helfrey. Ready when you are.

On December 23, 2006, Hurricane Sharon called. Dave and I were watching the movie *Down with Love* in the glow of the Christmas tree. It was around seven p.m.

"Wendy's in labor," Sharon said. "I'm at the hospital now, and I'll keep you posted on how things are going."

"So we shouldn't come down?" I asked, setting my drink on the table and starting to pace.

"No. Definitely don't come down. Wendy's kind of a mess right now, honestly. Just sit tight and I'll call when there's something to report."

I hung up the phone.

"What?" Dave asked.

"Nothing," I said. "We wait."

Big deep breaths. In through the nose, out through the mouth.

We called our families. We called the Coven. We called Dave's best friend Rob in California.

And then we waited.

Around eleven p.m. I called Sharon.

"Nothing to report," she said. "It's going slow. You guys should get some rest."

"How's Wendy?" I asked.

"She's doing okay. Her mom and dad are here."

Wendy had been estranged from her parents for some time, so I didn't know if that was a good thing or not.

"Go to bed," Sharon said. "I'll call if anything happens. I promise."

So we went to bed. I took two Benadryl to help me sleep. And as I laid my head on the cool, soft pillow, I was keenly aware of two things. The first: that this could very well be the last night of peaceful sleep Dave and I would have for a while. And the second: that I was lying comfortably in my bed while Wendy was in the hospital, laboring with my child.

We woke to the phone ringing at 6:15 on the morning of Christmas Eve.

"Ten pounds, two ounces," Sharon said. The trademark spark was missing from her voice. Then again, she'd been up all night. "He's super-healthy. Nine on the Apgar. Everything is perfect."

"So what do we do?" I asked. Dave was resting his chin on my shoulder, listening in.

"Umm, you guys need to sit tight for a while."

"Is something wrong?"

"Not necessarily. This is just a super-emotional time, and Wendy wants to be alone with the baby for as long as she can."

The agency has a mandatory twenty-four-hour waiting period before the birthmother is allowed to sign the relinquishment papers. This allows all the drugs to leave her system and ensures that she has a clear head when making the final decision. During the seminar, they told us that some birthmothers don't want to spend time with the baby, so the adoptive parents come to the hospital and stay in another room with the baby until the waiting period is over. But others want to have that time to say good-bye.

Or to change their minds.

We spent the day in a fog, bumping into each other in the hallway and the kitchen, halfheartedly sniping at each other, then collapsing into long, silent hugs. We were a mess.

Julie showed up in the afternoon with the curtains she'd just finished the night before, so we killed a couple of hours hanging them and primping the room. The crib was all made up, with soft animals lining the edges of the mattress and the wooden mobile hanging at the ready. The bassinet I'd borrowed from Pat back in July was stationed by my side of the bed. The baby monitor was charging. The car seat and fully packed diaper bag were sitting by the front door.

Around five o'clock I finally agreed to take a shower. I'd been shuffling around in my white terrycloth robe all day because I was afraid Sharon would call as soon as I stepped under the hot water. I didn't want to miss the call to come get my baby. I'd been waiting for that call for a long, long time.

At seven p.m. the phone finally rang.

"May I speak to Stacy or David, please?"

I didn't recognize the voice.

"This is Stacy," I said. Dave was again listening over my shoulder.

"Stacy, this is Meg Turner-Collins."

The Angry Hippie. Fran was on vacation. She was filling in.

"Hi, Meg."

"Yes. Hello. Stacy, I'm calling to let you know that Wendy and Josh have chosen to parent."

"They're keeping the baby?" I said. Dave sat down hard on the couch.

"They've chosen to parent, yes."

"Why? What happened?"

"Josh has agreed to help Wendy raise the child, and her parents have also stepped in and pledged their support."

But Josh didn't want to be a father. And Wendy hated her parents.

"Can we talk to her?"

"No, I'm sorry. That's not possible. Wendy wanted me to be sure to tell you that she was sorry, and that she hopes you get a baby soon."

"Are you fucking kidding me?" I said. It was the only logical thing left to say.

"I'm very sorry that you've experienced a disruption, but unfortunately, these things do happen."

Silence.

"Have a happy holiday, Stacy. We'll be in touch after the first of the year."

She hung up.

I don't really know how long Dave and I sat there in silence. But it seemed like a long time. Neither of us cried, I remember that much. Anger seemed like an appropriate emotion. But shock was all we could muster.

Eventually, Dave's hand crept over to mine and I grasped it.

"We have to tell people," I said.

When we were trying to get pregnant, we stopped telling people when we were going to have a procedure because it became too hard to tell them it didn't work. There were always a few exceptions, but for the most part, we kept our mouths shut. But now, with Wendy's baby, we had told everyone. Everyone.

And now we had to un-tell them.

CHAPTER EIGHTEEN

Merry Christmas

"We should've done IVF," I said as we drove down I-5. It was Christmas Day, and we were headed to my mom's house for dinner.

"IVF wasn't going to work for us," Dave said, one hand on my knee and the other on the steering wheel.

"We don't know that for sure," I said, staring out the window at the long stretches of farmland between Portland and Salem.

It was cold and gray. Snow would have been a nice distraction, but the forecast only called for rain.

Julie had called my brothers and told them there would be no baby. Everyone was expecting to meet a new nephew. Gifts had most likely been purchased. But when we got there, no one asked what had happened. No one said they were sorry. No one said a thing. They just pretended like nothing had happened.

That's my family.

Dave's family would have said something. They would have hugged us. They would have acknowledged our loss. And that's what it was: a loss. It wasn't, as Meg had said, a "disruption." It was a loss. It was our version of a miscarriage.

We left as soon as we possibly could.

Back home, I lay on the couch and watched *It's a Wonderful Life* while Dave went downstairs to e-mail all of our friends before they started calling to ask if they could come see the baby.

This is the e-mail he sent:

Hi again, everybody—

Well, it's been just shy of three weeks since I e-mailed you last about our adoption brouhaha, and the good news is, the wait is over! The bad news is, that's the only good news. Wendy and Josh exercised their option to keep their baby, who was lucky enough to come into the world yesterday.

So yeah, no baby for us this time around. We really do wish Wendy and Josh all the best luck in the world with their son, Logan. We really do. But as long as we're being honest here, we also wish we'd never met them, and that we never see them again.

For a while, I thought about not sending this bad news out at Christmas. Too much of a downer, you know? But obviously I rethought that. To start, this might bum you out for a few minutes, maybe an hour, but it's not like it's going to spoil your whole weekend. And it's CERTAINLY NOT because Stacy and I are throwing a pity party and want 75 people calling us and making cooing sounds. On the contrary.

The last thing I want to share with you is the hope that this Christmas, what just happened to Stacy and I might give you the perspective to love your own family just a little more this year.

Most people go through their lives assuming that having a family is a natural thing. Hey, guess what? It's not. It's hard fought and won. It's rare and precious and unfairly fragile. It has nothing to do with determination and everything to do with luck. I don't care if it's just you and your spouse; if your ex gets the kids on Christmas Eve and you don't get them until New Year's; if your kids are grown and strewn all over the country; if your babies are driving you batshit crazy, fighting over the better presents; if there are so many of you at dinner you have to cook two turkeys; or if your normal routine is to just sit there, silently chewing and counting the minutes until you can leave. Whatever you have—whether you're the Bradys or the Bundys—take stock in your luck and love it just a little more this year.

It'll be fun.

Merry Christmas—

Dave & Stacy

After the e-mail went out, our friends rallied around us in the way my family wasn't capable of. They called. They sent e-mails and flowers. They came by with pies and gin. We have the best friends.

The week between Christmas and New Year's is a mottled gray blur. I had arranged to take time off from work, thinking I was going to be a new mother. I probably should have gone back to work. I needed the money. But I just couldn't bring myself to write headlines for weight-loss solutions when all I wanted to do was scream, drink, and scream some more. So I took the week off and wallowed. But not before calling each and every one of my clients and telling them that there was no baby, and that I'd be available for work after the first of the year.

For New Year's Eve we had solid plans to do absolutely nothing, which our friends ruined by coming over and forcing us to celebrate. They brought food and champagne and board games, which turned out to be just the way to kill time between eight p.m. and midnight.

When the clock struck twelve, Dave and I held onto each other like two kids slow-dancing at the prom, and silently affirmed our predetermined mutual resolution: Won't Get Fooled Again.

CHAPTER NINETEEN

Happy New Year

In the middle of the second week in January, Dave and I drove to the agency to have a talk with Fran, who had returned from vacation and was eager to know what our next steps would be.

"How are you two?" she asked, after getting us coffee and water. We were in the room with the couches. The one where we'd met with Wendy and Josh. I'm sure she chose it because it was comfortable, but as far as we were concerned, it was the scene of the crime.

"Not so good," Dave answered.

"No, I imagine not," Fran said. "I'm so sorry, both of you."

"We want to make sure this never happens again," I said, crossing my arms in front of me.

"Well, if it makes you feel better, it's never happened before. Not in the history of this agency. We've never had an adoptive couple have two disruptions."

"No, it doesn't really make us feel better at all," Dave said. "And what's with this 'disruption' shit?"

Fran chuckled softly. "It's adoption-speak. People in the adoption community don't like to use negative words to describe birth-parents. It gets a little too PC sometimes."

"Okay, I get it," Dave said. "So changing your mind at the last freaking minute is 'choosing to parent,' and having our hearts ripped out and shown to us while they're still beating is called 'experiencing a disruption.' Is that right?"

"Well . . ."

"Just wanted to make sure I understood the lingo."

With the last part of that sentence, Dave employed what I like to call his Vicious Air Quotes. Trust me, they're vicious.

"I know that adoption-speak doesn't help you feel any better right now," Fran said. "It's just that there are a lot of old wounds from the way things used to be done."

"Yeah, well, there are a few new wounds, too," Dave said.

"Nothing about this process is easy," Fran said. "And I'm sorry you have to go through it."

Where had we heard that before?

"Does Wendy have to pay back the money you gave her?" Dave asked. He was itching for a fight.

"We never give any birthmother money directly," Fran explained. "But we do offer financial support. We help them pay their rent and medical bills, and we buy them groceries and clothes if they need it."

"Great. Does she have to pay you back?" Dave asked.

"No," Fran said.

"She played you, you know." Dave leaned back in his chair and crossed his arms. He reminded me of an angry teenager sitting in the principal's office.

"That may be true, but our policy is to let the birthparents keep whatever we give them, even if they change their minds. And for the record, I don't think that's what happened with Wendy."

"That's an astonishingly irresponsible policy," Dave countered. "Seriously. What's to stop every pregnant woman in town from coming to you, getting a free ride, and then 'choosing to parent' at the last minute?"

"David, if we asked for the money back, that would be financial coercion," Fran explained. "Can you see that? It would be the equivalent of paying her for her baby. We vet each birthmother very carefully before we ever introduce her to prospective parents. If we don't think they're serious about adoption, we steer them elsewhere. Now, I know this hurts, but the truth is, people change their minds. This is not a black-and-white situation. It's messy. And complicated. And sometimes people like you get hurt in the process."

Now Fran was the one leaning back in her chair with her arms crossed.

"Let's move on," I said, breaking up the fight before it could really get going. "Dave and I would like to change our birthparent preferences so we can avoid another Wendy and Josh situation."

Prior to throwing our hats into the adoption pool, Dave and I had filled out a Birthparent Preferences form. It specified things like age, marital status, smoking, drugs, and expectations about openness. Ours was intentionally vague because we didn't want to be too picky. We wanted to get chosen. The only thing we expressed any certainty about was drug use and drinking, and even then we said we would tolerate "some."

"What would you like to change?" Fran asked.

"No drug use. No drinking. No criminal background. And no father in the picture," I said, counting our demands off on each finger.

"Those are pretty narrow parameters. And not terribly realistic," she said.

"We don't want to go through this again," I said.

"I know you don't. And I don't want you to go through it again, either. But there's something you need to know," Fran said carefully.

"What? Wendy changed her mind again?" Dave said.

Fran laughed. "No. But you have been chosen again."

"That's not funny," Dave said.

"Well, it's a good thing I'm not kidding, then."

"Jesus," I said, to no one in particular.

"Would you like to hear about the birthmother who's chosen you?"

Dave and I looked at each other. And in that look was an unspoken conversation that went something like this:

Are you ready to do this again?

I don't know, are you ready?

I have no idea. But maybe this is the one, right?

Maybe. Maybe not. But I guess it's better than waiting.

Right. And what are the odds that something bad will happen again?

Let's not think about that.

So we'll do it?

Yeah. Let's do it.

— ◆ —

Birthmom #3 was named Audrey. She was in her mid-thirties and had two young kids. She was due to deliver a baby girl in March. She'd recently been homeless and knew she couldn't take on the financial burden of another child. She wanted an open adoption so her son and daughter could know their sister.

"Where's the father?" I asked. "What's her family situation?"

Cue Hurricane Sharon, who was, naturally, Audrey's case-worker. After showering us with bear hugs and you-poor-things, she settled in on one of the fluffy couches and gave us the details of Audrey's situation.

"Audrey's parents and sisters are pretty positive about the adoption. They're supporting her. The bigger problem is the baby's father," Sharon said.

Here we go.

"The father is Audrey's ex-husband, who is also the father of her other two kids. They were married at the time the baby was conceived, which means he has full parental rights and has to sign the relinquishment form in order for the adoption to go through."

"And he doesn't want to sign?" I asked.

"It's not so much that he doesn't want to sign," Sharon said. "It's that he's in prison."

Awesome.

Audrey's ex was in prison for beating her up while she was pregnant with this child. It was his third strike, so he got a three-year sentence. Because they couldn't have just thrown him in prison for knocking his pregnant wife around. He had to have done it three times.

"So what are we worried about?" I asked. "If he's in prison, he can't do anything about it, right?"

"He still has parental rights, and he has to sign the papers if the adoption is going to go through," Fran said.

"Yeah, but he's *in prison*," Dave said, struggling to hold back the "Duh."

"Doesn't matter," Sharon said. "He's the legal father."

"Okay, so what do we think he's going to do?" I asked.

"Audrey thinks he'll sign," Sharon said. "She's made it clear that if he wants to have any contact with his other two kids once he gets out, he needs to sign the papers."

"But that's coercion," I said.

"That only applies to the mother," Fran said.

"Seriously?" Dave asked.

"Seriously," said Sharon. "I'm going out to the prison tomorrow to meet with him. I'll get a better sense of where he's coming from then. In the meantime, you guys need to think about what you want to do here. I'd understand if you said no, considering everything you've been through. But for what it's worth, I think this one is going to work out."

"You're not going to show the father our family book, are you?" I asked.

"No. Definitely not. I'm just going to give him a general sense of who you guys are. No specifics."

"And the open-adoption agreement? If this goes through, does the agreement apply to him, too? Would we be expected to meet with him?"

"Not if you don't want to," Sharon said. "We can specify that as part of the agreement."

"We don't want this person in our lives," Dave said. "At all. We don't want him to know our names, where we live, nothing."

"I'll talk to him tomorrow and let you know what happens," Sharon said. "In the meantime, do you want to meet Audrey?"

"If we say yes, does that mean we've committed?" Dave asked.

"No. You can decide after you meet her," Sharon said.

"Then yes," I said. "Let's meet her and go from there."

CHAPTER TWENTY

Back in the Saddle Again

"I have absolutely no idea how to feel right now," I said, opening a bottle of wine. Dave and I were standing in our kitchen, with the bright January light streaming in, giving the illusion of warmth. We'd just gotten home from our meeting with Fran. From where I was standing, I could see down the hall to the nursery. The wooden mobile was just visible beyond the doorway. When we bought it, Dave and I were so sure we'd gotten past the worst of it. Infertility had been a nightmare. Adoption would be a dream.

"We just need to keep our guard up this time," he said, pouring himself a Diet Coke. "We can't get sucked in emotionally."

"How the hell are we going to do that?" I asked. "We're talking about adopting someone's baby. It's nothing *but* emotion."

"Birthmothers change their minds," he said. "We know that now. The only power we have is over ourselves."

"We must remain vigilant," I said, in my best George W. Bush voice.

"You laugh, but I'm really kinda serious here."

"I know," I said. "But what's the harm in meeting her?"

"The harm is that we get sucked in again," he said, taking a long swallow. "That we get suckered again."

"I told you we should have listened to my family," I said. "Why try if there's a chance you could fail? Saves a person so much trouble."

"There's no shame in quitting," Dave said, mimicking my mother's solemnity.

"See? You're getting it. You'll be a real Bolt yet."

—— ——

We met Audrey on a gray afternoon in early February. It was the same room with the big couches. The room where Wendy had lied to us over and over. I was nervous, but not in the same way as I had been with Wendy. Now, instead of worrying about being rejected, I was wondering if I was going to have to tell an abused pregnant woman that I didn't want her baby. But thanks anyway.

I went in with my armor on.

She had black hair and dark eyes, and a soft, trusting face that wasn't quite right. Maybe it was the pregnancy hormones. Or water retention. Or maybe she'd been punched a lot. But her features seemed to be just slightly askew, as if someone had very subtly rearranged the furniture.

She pushed herself out of the chair and hugged me. She was farther along than Wendy had been the first time we'd met her, but Audrey's belly was nowhere near as big.

"I'm so glad you guys came," she said. "I was afraid you wouldn't want to. But I didn't want to meet any other parents. As soon as I saw your book, I knew you were the ones."

Audrey's words came spilling out of her like water into a bathtub. She'd been waiting for this meeting. Looking forward to it, even. Audrey wasn't thinking it over, weighing her options. She wanted this.

She told us she'd done some coke early in her pregnancy, before she knew. But after that, she'd been clean. She'd paid dearly for her decision to prosecute and divorce her husband. He was a violent asshole, but he paid the bills. After he went to prison, Audrey struggled to support her two kids, but she eventually went under. They'd been living in their car when Audrey contacted the agency. Another baby, Audrey told us, wouldn't be fair to her son and daughter. They'd already given up so much. And she was in no position to take on the responsibility.

"What's the story with the father?" Dave asked abruptly. He was still wearing his armor. Mine was in a pile over by the door. "Because none of this matters if he doesn't sign, right?" Dave was looking at Sharon and Fran.

"Both Audrey and her ex-husband have to sign the relinquishment papers, yes," said Fran.

"I've spoken to him a couple of times now, and I really think he's going to sign," said Sharon, who had said the same thing of Wendy. Her opinion was irrelevant.

"He'll do it," Audrey said quietly.

The room was quiet for moment until Dave spoke.

"Audrey, I'm really sorry for everything you've been through,"

Dave said gently, leaning forward to get Audrey's attention. "Your ex-husband deserves to have a candiru fish invade his urethra for what he's done to you and your kids. He's an abusive shit. Which, unfortunately for everyone in this room, means he's probably also a liar."

"He'll sign," Audrey repeated calmly. "If I have to go there and talk to him, I will. But he will sign."

Two days after meeting Audrey, I found myself in the Baby Girls' section at Old Navy. Before I even realized what I was doing, I'd bought three frilly spring dresses, newborn size. As I drove out of the parking lot, I kept glancing at the bag on the passenger seat, trying to put a name to the feelings I was having. Then I remembered: It was the ghost of hubris, leftover from my days of trying to conceive. *I'd jinxed it by buying the dresses,* I thought. Now it would never work out. *No, that's not true,* I told myself from another part of my brain, a part that had no use for those feelings. These dresses are for Audrey, I told myself. I'll just give them to her the next time I see her. That will prove that I'm not emotionally connected to her baby. And that will make everything work out.

This was a desperately fucked-up situation.

———

February ticked by slowly. We told only a few people this time: my sister Julie, Dave's parents, one or two friends. There was no real news as far as Audrey's husband was concerned. He told Sharon he would "probably" sign the papers, but he couldn't really know until the time came. He wanted to have control over Audrey for as long as he possibly could.

Audrey went past her due date and her amniotic-fluid levels were decreasing, so her doctor decided to induce her on a Friday morning. The baby was born early Saturday, healthy and perfect. Audrey wanted Dave and me to come to the hospital to meet her, but Sharon and Fran told us not to. Because it was a weekend, the prison officials who needed to be there to witness the signing of the papers weren't there, so the earliest he could be served the papers would be Monday morning. Audrey was due to be discharged on Sunday. That meant one of two things was going to happen: Either the baby would go home with Audrey, or she'd be put into foster care until the adoption could be worked out. Audrey didn't want to take the baby home because she didn't want to complicate things for her two other kids. But no one, including Audrey, wanted the baby to go into foster care. And even though Dave and I were ready and willing to take her home, we couldn't. We had no rights.

So Audrey took the baby home and we all waited for Monday to come.

The sun came out on Monday, Dave's birthday. He passed the time out in the garden, turning the soil and putting a few hardy plants in the ground. I sat at my computer and fretted, opening and closing the photo Sharon had e-mailed me on Saturday. It was Audrey holding the baby. The picture had been her idea. She wanted us to see the baby, to have a connection to her. She was afraid we were going to change our minds. But it was way too late for that. We'd already named her Annabelle, after my favorite aunt. She had thick black hair and a squishy baby face that was a miniature version of her mother's. Audrey's son and daughter were piled into the hospital bed with her and all four of them were looking at the camera as if to say, "We're your new family." And they would be. All four of them would be in our lives for the rest of our lives. And we were good with that.

It was three o'clock by the time Fran called us and said the three words that were not a surprise, but still knocked the breath out of me.

"He won't sign," she said quietly.

I wondered how long Fran had known this news and just couldn't bring herself to deliver it.

He didn't want strangers raising his child, she told me. He'd get out in a year, and when he did, he was going to sue Audrey for custody. He never had any intention of signing, he'd told Sharon with a smile. He just wanted Audrey to have to sweat it out.

So, to recap: The mother of the baby wanted us to adopt the baby, we wanted to adopt the baby, but because some abusive shit heel just happened to be legally married to the mother when he knocked her up, he ended up controlling the entire situation. And no one got what they wanted but him.

After I hung up with Fran, I sat at my desk and held my face in my hands. I breathed deeply, waiting for the tears to come. Surely, there would be tears this time? But there was nothing but hard emptiness and a growing sense that I had wasted the last four years of my life.

I went out to the backyard where Dave was working and I put my arms around him from behind. I didn't say anything as I rested my cheek on the middle of his sweaty back.

"You've got to be fucking kidding me," he said, turning around to look me in the eye.

I shook my head and he sat down hard in the dirt, throwing his hand trowel toward the fence.

"Motherfucker," he said.

That night we observed Dave's birthday with Amy and Roland and Julie. They were among the few people who knew about Audrey's baby and had helped see us through the loss of Wendy and Josh's baby a few months earlier. They knew the territory. We drank a lot, ate fried chicken, and picked at a sheet cake I'd ordered earlier in the week. In a display of shockingly poor judgment on my part, I had asked the bakery to decorate the cake with the words HAPPY BIRTHDAY, POPS. After several cocktails, but before we presented the cake to Dave, my sister and I changed it to read HAPPY BIRTHDAY, POOPS.

Later, after everyone had left, Dave and I lay in bed and tried to process what had happened to us, again.

"This is a sign," I told him. "It's a sign that we aren't meant to be parents."

It was something that had been rattling around in my head for a while. I wasn't much for religion, or even spirituality. But if the universe was capable of giving signs, this one seemed pretty clear.

Dave was silent for a long time.

"Maybe it's not a sign," he said, finally. "Maybe it's a test."

CHAPTER TWENTY-ONE

Humoring Crazy People

People often ask me why Dave and I kept going. Why didn't we give up, they wondered. And it was a reasonable question, the answer to which was simple: We would have, if we'd had time.

Two days after we lost Annabelle, Fran called.

"I know you two are hurting right now, and if you say no to this, I will understand completely," she said.

"Fran, you cannot possibly be calling to tell me there's another baby," I said. I was sitting at my computer doing some quick research on whether or not it's a felony to mail a box of cat feces to a prisoner.

"Well, yes. I am," she said. "But this one is different. Just listen."

There were a lot of details to absorb about Cathy (birthmother #4, for those of you keeping track at home). But the ones I chose to focus on were these: She had no family. She didn't want to meet us. And she wanted no contact before or after the papers were signed. Ever.

Those were the only things that mattered to me. The rest was just background noise.

"Okay, let me see if I got everything," Dave said. He was standing in the kitchen with me, guzzling a Diet Coke. I had just gotten off the phone with Fran. "Cathy is a forty-year-old heroin addict who had no prenatal care until a week ago and is due to be induced in three days. Is that right?"

"Well, technically, she's a recovering heroin addict," I offered, helpfully.

"Right, right. So she's on methadone or something?"

"Suboxone," I said. "And why are you talking so slowly?"

"Because that's how you talk to crazy people."

"I'm not crazy," I said, unconvincingly.

"You are if you think we're going to adopt this baby."

"Dave. There might not be anything wrong. He might be just fine."

"Might be."

"Right. And she doesn't want any contact. Ever. And she doesn't have any crazy family members or ex-husbands who are going to swoop in at the last minute and fuck things up. It's perfect."

"If this is what 'perfect' has come to look like, we need to take a break."

"Just talk to the doctor with me. Fran says Cathy consented to let us talk to her doctor. Let's get more information before we write this baby off. Please?"

More information didn't help. Cathy's doctor was a very nice, very blunt man who told us he was inducing a month before her due date because the neonatal intensive care unit was a safer place for the baby than his mother's womb. He also told us that Cathy had been taking Klonopin for anxiety throughout her pregnancy and that she had tested positive for cocaine a week earlier.

"At the absolute minimum," the doctor told us, "this baby will be born addicted to the Klonopin and will need to go through withdrawal before he can go home. There's a chance he'll also be addicted to the Suboxone, but we don't know for sure. It's a newer drug, and we still don't know what the long-term effects are for a child whose mother took the drug while pregnant."

"And the coke?" Dave asked. "What's the effect there?"

"Hard to say. I don't know if she used it for the first time a week ago, or if she's been using throughout her pregnancy."

"Let's assume it's the latter," Dave said. "What's the story?"

"Baby will be born addicted, for sure," the doctor said. "Long-term, you're looking at behavioral problems, learning disabilities, that kind of thing. Plus, the chance that he'll have addiction issues when he grows up is pretty high."

I was listening on the downstairs phone; Dave was upstairs. I hung up. I didn't want to hear any more.

About twenty minutes later, Dave came down and put his hand on my shoulder.

"I'm sorry, sweetie. I know you wanted this to work out," he said.

"Marie's sister is a pediatrician. I have an e-mail in to her."

"Uh-huh."

"And I'm going to call Dr. Collins."

"Who's Dr. Collins?" Dave asked.

"Our pediatrician," I said.

"Why do we have a pediatrician when we don't have a child?"

"We're going to have one, so we need a pediatrician. Pat recommended her."

"Okay. And what is it you're going to call her about?"

"About the baby."

"What baby?"

"Cathy's baby. Our baby."

Long silence. Dave was visibly angry and struggling to get it under control before he spoke.

"We're not adopting this baby," he said finally, quietly.

"Why not?" I asked. Because I really wanted to know.

"Did you hear anything the doctor just told us?"

"Of course I did. But I don't think it's hopeless. This could work."

Dave kneeled down beside my chair. "Why are you doing this?" he asked. Because he really wanted to know.

"Why aren't you?" I snapped.

"Because it's insane! Why can't you see that?"

"Maybe it is insane. But it's our only chance," I said. "We have run out of chances, Dave. Everyone else has changed their minds. This woman is not going to change her mind. She doesn't want this baby. She doesn't care about this baby. She's not going to change her mind."

Dave stood up. "Okay," he said. "Let's talk to some more people."

"Thank you," I said, watching him go up the stairs alone.

And so we talked: to pediatricians, to the March of Dimes, to Fran, and to each other. And they all told us the same thing—addiction, withdrawal, NICU, and a big, long-term question mark.

The last person we talked to was our friend John, Pat's husband and a pediatrician. Again we listened in on different floors. John told us what I had been thinking, but was afraid to say out loud: This child was going to be a special-needs child. And were we sure we wanted that? Were we ready for what that might mean? And the answer—sadly, disappointingly—was no. And that, right there, that ugly truth, was why we were never going to be parents: because we didn't deserve it. Because I didn't deserve it. And I never should have tried in the first place.

Once again I hung up the phone before the conversation was over, but this time it was because I didn't want John or Dave to hear me crying. And boy, did I cry. Deep, gasping sobs came up from inside me where they'd been festering for all this time. And now, finally, I let them out. Because it was over. All of it. Over.

After Dave got off the phone with John, he came downstairs and cried with me. I don't know how long we stayed down there like that. But when we were done, I went upstairs and took one last look at the nursery—fully stocked with clothes and diapers and lotions and soft, Easter egg–colored animals. It was March 30. Nine months since we had first thrown our names into the adoption pool. The irony of that washed over me as I closed the door behind me.

That was the end of that.

CHAPTER TWENTY-TWO

Love Poems and Chili

The next morning, I felt clear and new and raw. A weight had been lifted off and replaced with a new one. What would the rest of our lives look like? We weren't going to be parents; that much we knew. But we'd spent so much of the last five years trying to make that happen, it was nearly impossible to see a future without a child in it. That would take time, I guessed.

I called Fran at home. It was Saturday morning. She wasn't surprised that we'd decided not to adopt Cathy's baby. And she wasn't surprised that we were done with adoption. She was just sorry, for the whole thing.

"I know you would have been great parents," she said. I thought she might have been crying a little.

"Will there be someone else to take him?" I asked.

"Oh yes," she said. "Bob and Laura are ready to step in. They're naturals."

Bob and Laura were the Show-Offs from our orientation weekend, nearly a year ago. The people who wanted to spend their retirement years caring for special-needs kids. They were naturals. They didn't think twice about adopting a drug-addicted baby.

Fran and I said our good-byes and I went to do what had become a habit: call family and friends with the bad news. But there was no one to call this time. We hadn't told anyone about Cathy's baby. We'd learned our lesson, I guess.

"What do we do now?" I asked Dave. He was staring out our dining-room window, through glass so old it was warped. The trees in our front yard were starting to show signs of life.

"I guess we do whatever we'd be doing if none of this had ever happened," he said. "I think I'm going to put that new rhody in the ground."

We'd bought a new rhododendron bush called "Love Poem" a few weeks back. It had soft, coral-colored flowers. I don't usually like rhodies because they're so freaking common in Oregon. But this one was such an unusual color, and we had a big hole in the front yard where Dave had dug up an ancient lavender bush in a fit of misplaced anger after Audrey's ex-husband had refused to sign the papers. This seemed like the perfect day for filling up a gaping hole.

While Dave got his gardening clothes on, I called up some friends to arrange a game night. Roland, Amy, and Marie. *Let's get drunk and play Scattergories*, I thought. That's normal.

I started to gather the ingredients for a big pot of chili when the phone rang. Dave grabbed the downstairs extension. When he came up the stairs a few minutes later, he was laughing.

"Did Marie forget that she had something else to do tonight?" I asked. This was typical of Marie.

"Umm, no," he said slowly. "That was Fran."

"Why? Is something wrong with Cathy's baby?"

"No. There's another baby. It's being born right now."

Dave was running his fingers through his dark, curly hair. It was grayer than when we'd started all this. And thinner.

"Right, and in about twenty minutes the birthmother is going to change her mind," I laughed. Bitter, bitter, bitter.

"Yeah, probably," he said.

"What did you tell her?"

"I told her we weren't going to go through this again, so she shouldn't call back unless it was real," he said.

"Good," I said. "Thank you."

"Do you want to—"

"No. I don't. I don't want to know anything. Go plant your bush."

The chili is from a recipe my friend Lorena gave me. It's a complex mixture of spices—everything from cumin and cayenne to cinnamon and cocoa powder. It takes forever to make, and uses up every spice in the cabinet, but it's so worth it.

It had been simmering for almost three hours when Fran called back.

"I know you're hurting right now," she said, before I could say anything. "But I need to talk to you."

"I don't want to hear this, Fran. I don't. I will not do this again. Please don't ask me to."

"I would never have called you if I didn't know it was the real thing," she said.

"What does that mean?"

"It means, I think you need to come down here and meet your son."

Dave was on his knees in the front yard, patting the earth down around the new rhododendron.

"Honey," I said.

He turned around to look at me, then stood up, brushing the mud from his pants.

"Fran says we need to come to the hospital," I said.

He looked at me for a long time, studying my face.

"Let me go change my clothes," he said.

On the drive out to the hospital, I told Dave what Fran had told me: A twenty-six-year-old woman had walked into Willamette Falls Hospital in active labor and told the admitting nurse that she needed to arrange for an adoption. The nurse knew someone who worked at our agency, so she called them. Hurricane Sharon came down and talked to the mother, then called Fran and told her to call us.

The baby was born at 3:10 p.m. on March 31. Seven pounds, eight ounces. He scored a nine on the Apgar test, and his drug screen came out clean, as did the mother's.

The mother didn't want any contact with us. She didn't want to meet us or know our names. And she didn't want any contact with the baby. Ever. Sharon was fully convinced that she would go through with the adoption.

But Sharon had been sure before.

When we got to the hospital's maternity ward, we told the front-desk nurses that we were there to see Fran.

"The adoption," one of them whispered to the other.

One of the nurses led us down a wide, quiet hallway to a room where Fran was waiting for us. It was a birthing suite, with a big tub and a bed and lots of comfy chairs scattered all around. I remember feeling almost criminally out of place.

"Are you ready?" Fran asked, smiling.

"Are you sure?" Dave asked her. "Like, really sure?"

"I am," she said.

Fran left the room and Dave grabbed my hand tight.

"What's happening?" he asked.

"I have no idea," I answered, honestly.

Fran came back into the room a few minutes later, followed by the same nurse who had been at the front desk. She was pushing a rolling cart with blankets in it. I remember thinking, *Why is she bringing us blankets?*

As she got closer, I saw him. He was wrapped, burrito-style, in a white flannel blanket with pink and blue stripes. On his head was a blue-and-white-striped knit cap. So unbelievably tiny. He was sleeping.

The nurse picked him up and held him out to me.

"Would you like to hold him?" she asked.

Of all the babies we had almost adopted, I'd never held a single one of them.

"Can I?" I asked Fran.

"Of course you can," she answered.

"Should I?"

"Yes. Definitely."

He woke up when the nurse handed him to me. His grayish-blue eyes moved languidly from left to right and finally landed on mine. We stared into each other's eyes for what felt like nine months.

"What took you so long?" I asked him.

CHAPTER TWENTY-THREE

April Fools

When we returned home, our friends were waiting for us with a bottle of champagne. Before we'd left for the hospital, I had asked Amy and Roland to come over and stir the chili while we were gone. Because that's important, right? The chili?

We'd kept them updated via text message while we were at the hospital, so they knew things had gone well enough to warrant some mid-priced champagne. Save the good stuff for after the papers are signed, we told them.

At the hospital, Fran told us that we would have to wait twenty-four hours before the baby's mother could legally sign the adoption papers. A doctor and a nurse would have to sign an affidavit stating that she had no drugs in her system and was mentally competent to make the decision to sign away her parental rights forever. No take-backs.

After being assured that the baby would be well cared for and would likely sleep most of the night, we left after each of us had had a chance to hold him and kiss him and smell his sweet head.

We sat around the living room with our friends for a couple of hours, but then shooed them out around ten o'clock. Somewhere in all the ridiculous ups and downs of that day, we were vaguely aware that we were looking at our last night of peaceful sleep for quite some time.

The next morning, we packed a bag of tiny clothes, installed the car seat in Dave's car, and drove back out to the hospital as early as we possibly could. A new nurse set us up in the same birthing suite as the night before and then rolled in the baby, this time with a pale blue pacifier in his mouth.

Fran arrived. Then Sharon. Dave and I had agreed the night before that we wouldn't call our families until it was official. So it was just the five of us, waiting.

It was April first. April Fools' Day. A fact that was lost on no one.

As the hours passed, the nurse showed us how to bottle-feed him, and burp him, and change his diaper. She showed me how to wrangle his tiny limbs into the soft onesie we'd brought. Every time she came in, she'd slip me another piece of advice the way my dad used to slip me twenty-dollar bills back in college. Make sure you hold the bottle like this, or else he'll get gas. Some people think you need to warm up the formula, but you really don't. If you wrap him up tight, he'll be less likely to get fussy.

I loved that nurse.

As morning turned to afternoon, Fran and Sharon left us

alone for a while. While the baby slept, Dave and I decided to name him Xander Bolt Helfrey.

It was strange knowing that the birthmother was in the same hospital right at the same time. What must she be thinking? What was she going through? Was she relieved? Or heartbroken? What did she look like?

Around three o'clock, Fran and Sharon came back in, smiling. Fran thrust a stack of papers at us. "It's time to sign," she said.

Dave and I looked at each other, then back at Fran.

"She signed?" I asked.

"She did," Fran answered. "Just now."

Four times we'd been at this point. Three times a birthparent had refused to sign. Once, it was us who refused. This time, the fifth time, it had actually happened.

I don't remember how many papers we had to sign, but I do remember thinking that it wasn't as many as when we'd bought our house.

When the last page had been signed and dated, we found ourselves crushed in a giant bear hug by Hurricane Sharon. When she pulled away, her face was wet with tears.

"I am so glad this story got to have a happy ending," she said, wiping her wet face with the back of her hand.

For our part, Dave and I were remarkably calm. Clearly, the reality had yet to hit us. But for the moment, we had fun calling our parents and sisters and brothers and saying the same thing each time: "Guess what I'm doing right now?" *What?* they'd ask, expecting nothing in particular. "Holding my son," we'd say. And then we'd tell the story over and over again.

As the afternoon went on, people started arriving at the hospital. My sister Julie, the Coven, Roland, and Amy. They brought stuffed animals and flowers and, most important, lunch.

For a while, the nurse took the baby out to "have more tests." Totally normal, she told us. Be back in a bit. She returned him about thirty minutes later and it was then that Fran told us the birthmother had asked to see the baby. To say good-bye.

"Can I see her?" I wanted to know. "Can I thank her?"

"No," Fran told me. "She's already gone."

Around six o'clock, the hospital discharged the baby to us. By that time, everyone had left and it was just us three. We were a family. We had a son. Dave was a father. I was a mother. Twenty-four hours earlier, that had not been true. But now it was.

I stood in the lobby waiting for Dave to bring the car around. Xander was tucked into his car seat, sucking on his pacifier. My favorite nurse stood and waited with me, staring out the sliding doors at a spring sunset: dark gray and bright pink and fiery orange all mixed together.

Dave's black Subaru pulled up to the entrance. The nurse, whose name I can't remember, touched my shoulder and said, "Time to go, Mama." It was the first time someone called me that.

I thanked her for everything, then carried my son through the parting doors. I looked behind me as the doors swished closed, half expecting someone to come running through them telling me to stop. There had been a mistake. She'd changed her mind. April Fools!

But no one did.

Acknowledgments

First and foremost, I'd like to offer buckets of gratitude to my literary godmothers, Cheryl Strayed and Karen Karbo (aka, Sugar & Spice). Having to show up at your respective homes with new pages every month is an excellent way for a serial procrastinator to get a book written. I highly recommend it. To David Biespiel and the Attic Institute, for giving me the opportunity to work with such amazing mentors. To the fabulous Chelsea Cain, who saw this book in outline form long before I knew how it would end, and always had faith in it. To my agent, Joy Harris, for listening to Chelsea and taking a chance on me. And to my fearless editor, Lara Asher, who believed in this book and helped bring it into the world.

I'm ridiculously lucky to have friends like Marie Murphy, Katie Miller Lyman, Pat Janowski, Courtenay Hameister, Adam Murdoch, Christopher Bateman, Amy Taramasso, Roland Gauthier, Scott Poole, Ryan White, Rachel Bachmann, and Greg Robillard. Thank you for your faith, encouragement, and bottomless liquor cabinets. Thank you to Robyn Tenenbaum and Kate Sokoloff, for continuing to give me a microphone. Thanks to my big sister Julie, who has always been in my corner, even though I got braces and she didn't. And most of all, thanks to my husband and best friend, David Helfrey, for absolutely everything. RIP, Elvis.

About the Author

Stacy Bolt has never written a book before. She does not have an MFA, a fancy fellowship, or a Man Booker Prize. But she does have a job writing copy for an advertising agency, where the benefits are excellent and the bar is well stocked. When her bosses aren't looking, she writes personal essays that have been featured on *Live Wire*, a nationally syndicated radio program. She wrote this book during a long string of late nights and early mornings, and she really hopes you like it. Stacy lives in Portland, Oregon, with her husband and son.